When

COLORBLINDNESS
ISN'T THE ANSWER

Humanism in Practice

Series Editor
Anthony B. Pinn
Rice University
Institute for Humanist Studies (Washington, DC)

Humanism in Practice presents books concerned with what humanism says about contemporary issues. Written in a reader-friendly manner, the books in this series challenge readers to reflect on human values and how they impact our current circumstances.

When
COLORBLINDNESS
ISN'T THE ANSWER

Humanism and the Challenge of Race

ANTHONY B. PINN

PITCHSTONE PUBLISHING
Durham, North Carolina

and

INSTITUTE FOR HUMANIST STUDIES
Washington, DC

Pitchstone Publishing
Durham, North Carolina
www.pitchstonepublishing.com

Institute for Humanist Studies
Washington, DC
www.humaniststudies.org

10 9 8 7 6 5 4 3 2 1

Library of Congress Cataloging-in-Publication Data

Names: Pinn, Anthony B., author.
Title: When colorblindness isn't the answer : humanism and the challenge of
    race / Anthony B. Pinn.
Description: Durham, North Carolina : Pitchstone Publishing ; Washington, DC
    : Institute for Humanist Studies, [2017] | Series: Humanism in practice
Identifiers: LCCN 2016052927| ISBN 9781634311229 (paperback) | ISBN
    9781634311243 (epdf) | ISBN 9781634311250 (mobi)
Subjects: LCSH: Humanism—United States. | Humanism, Religious. |
    Race--Religious aspects. | United States—Race relations—Religious
    aspects. | BISAC: SOCIAL SCIENCE / Ethnic Studies / African American
    Studies. | PHILOSOPHY / Movements / Humanism.
Classification: LCC B821 .P473 2017 | DDC 144—dc23
LC record available at https://lccn.loc.gov/2016052927

CONTENTS

* * *

ACKNOWLEDGMENTS

* * *

The idea for this book and the series of which it is a part stem from a panel discussion at one of the American Humanist Association annual meetings. I want to thank the staff of the American Humanist Association, particularly Maggie Ardiente, and the editor of *The Humanist*, Jennifer Bardi, for their encouragement and willingness to give the ideas presented in these pages their first hearing. Thanks also to Drs. Sikivu Hutchinson, Monica Miller, and Christopher Driscoll for participating in that panel discussion and for the insights they shared. As always, I want to thank family and friends—particularly, in this case, Herb and Linda Kelly for their good humor and much needed time away from the computer. I must also thank the Institute for Philosophical Research (Hannover, Germany) for space to write and important conversations regarding humanism.

The idea wouldn't have survived the plane ride home and a few minutes of thought in my office if not for Kurt Volkan. Thanks, Kurt! Finally, I must offer my thanks to *Free Inquiry* for permission to reprint an essay first published in that journal (now chapter seven in this volume).

When

COLORBLINDNESS
ISN'T THE ANSWER

INTRODUCTION

* * *

There are debates, heated discussions really, within the humanist "movement" (of which I consider myself a part) revolving around the agenda that should guide humanist thinking and activism.

Is it enough to address separation of church and state? Of course, science education should be high on the list of key issues meriting humanist time and resources, right? And, public policy is certainly the context in which reason and logic are celebrated and highlighted as necessary for the proper working of democracy. This, as an element of humanist activism, is a given, correct? These are just a few examples of the activism possibilities that receive energetic conversation and attention within the humanist circles familiar to me. Such issues and debate, in a significant way, have shaped the public presence and "look" of humanism for some time now.

One can think about these issues I've mentioned as marking out how humanists understand their world and interact with that world. That is to say, such issues or platforms have something to do with the interactions of humanists individually and within the context of collectives called communities, social groupings, and so on. But these platforms, at least for some of us, raise the question: what does humanism have to say to and about those bodies at work within both private and public realms? Let me explain why I bring up bodies and what I mean to suggest by this attention to bodies.

Without getting too philosophical, these bodies are material (i.e., born, live, and die), but we also know them as social constructs or a type of cultural "thing." That is to say, by the latter point, what we know about our bodies is determined by what we can speak (through language) about these bodies. I suggest humanists understand without significant trouble or confusion the material—biological— reality of bodies. However, humanists have a more difficult time understanding and addressing the social construction of these bodies.

The former—the biological reality—bends to logic and science, while the social construction of bodies has no necessary logic and isn't defined by the assumed "objective" findings of science. Perhaps it is this differentiation between material and social bodies prompting some to argue social issues—such as racism—aren't fundamental to humanism and its activists? In a word, the position for some goes this way: if science doesn't hold the key to understanding an issue, or if logic and reason alone cannot address an issue, then that issue isn't a pressing concern for humanists.

Despite the thinking I've suggested above, so many of the speaking invitations I receive from humanist organizations and communities revolve around questions not guided by a "scientific," "it's-got-to-be-reasonable" approach to engagement. These questions seek—albeit in sloppy ways—to recognize socially constructed bodies as bodies worthy of attention: How do we get more African Americans into the movement? Or, why are so many African Americans still involved in a religious tradition (i.e., Christianity) that was used to enslave them and that continues to justify racial discrimination, among other modes of injustice? Both questions point out an example of the social significance of race—and its enactment in the mode of racism—while also suggesting a desire—at least on the part of some—to address race as a humanist issue.

I am one who has argued for a few decades now that humanism should address issues of social injustice, like racism, as part of its commitment to the well-being of life in general and human flourishing in particular. To omit attention to modes of social injustice—like racism—is to reduce the connotations of the human in *human*ism. Furthermore, it is to truncate the challenges confronting human well-being in the contemporary world. And so, I typically accept invitations to talk about humanism and race, and to offer historical perspective and prospects. Those lectures take a good amount of time out of my schedule. And, as I make my way from the stage to the hallway, the exchanges postlecture add a good number of minutes to my interactions with humanist community members. I have no complaints about the time I spend talking about humanism and race. I'm glad to give those presentations.

Yet, recent conversations concerning a definition of humanism and its mission motivate me to offer something more concise, certainly more condensed and "bite-size" then the talks and lectures. At one American Humanist Association (AHA) annual gathering my effort to provide a thumbnail platform on social injustice took the form of a list of "don'ts and dos" for humanists interested in issues of race and racism. I think it's worth sharing in greater detail some of those thoughts and challenges.

Of course, it goes without saying, but these chapters, and themes contained in them, aren't the only plausible or even necessary points to consider when addressing racial justice. What I offer here, naturally, is incomplete. However, telling readers everything they need to know isn't really the goal of this book, or the other books in this series. In fact, not every racial group is covered in this volume; and, this may be a point of contention for some readers. The tone isn't "academic," that is to say I avoid jargon. It is intended to have a reader-friendly "feel"— one marked by a flow of prose meant to encourage conversation.

It's important to say a word concerning the audience for this book. While I certainly have white Americans in mind, the intended audience isn't limited to that group. Racial minorities, I believe, will also benefit from reading this book if for no other reason than it will force them to think beyond the circumstances of their particular group and its collective experience as *the* marker of race and racial injustice. It will be of benefit to humanists and those who don't claim humanism in that both theistic and humanistic viewpoints tell us something about what it means to live in the United States; and, we do well to know something about these various perspectives. In short, I hope to provide food for thought for a range of humanists and nonhumanist readers—those who believe themselves to live at a distance from racial issues, those who understand themselves to be impacted by race/racism, and those who aren't certain where they fit into the discussion. Black, white, brown, yellow, red, tan . . . it doesn't matter for the purposes of this book. Living in the United States with all that entails makes race/racism a topic we all need to discuss.

Again, this book isn't meant as an encyclopedic discussion of race and racism in the United States, covering the sweeping history of race as a mark of personhood, or lack thereof. No. Rather, I present ideas as icebreakers, so to speak, encouraging greater attention to and disciplined praxis (i.e., action based on deep thought and reflection) concerning the nature and meaning of race *in the United States* from a humanist vantage point. Read it. Wrestle with the ideas, and engage with race where and how you are able—helping to achieve a reasonable world more free from racial injustice.

SECTION ONE

Understanding the Impact of Race

1

BLANKET STATEMENTS ON RACE AND THEISM

Why does your community embrace religious traditions that have been used to do harm?

* * *

You'll notice that I use the term "theism" over against the more common concern of humanists and atheists—"religion." This is an intentional move on my part, one meant to point out what I would consider the actual target of humanist/atheist critique and challenge. In a word, both "secular" humanists and atheists argue there is no evidence sufficient to advance the idea of God or gods. They oppose the reality of an overarching force in the world that shapes and orchestrates creation and ongoing life (and death)—called God or gods and addressed through a variety of names: Allah, Jehovah, Changó, Krishna, and so on. Theologians, like Paul Tillich, have argued that "God" serves for theists as the "ultimate concern" that determines the shape of life—what is done, what isn't done, and what motivates us as we move along this pathway of ethics and morals. One should not assume this pathway only goes in the direction of well-being and healthy conduct. No, as human history demonstrates, allegiance to the will of God or gods can lead to destructive behavior and violent attitudes.

It is willingness to be guided by an imaginary force that troubles humanists, and the destructive and otherwise counterproductive thinking and behavior stemming from this allegiance gets the brunt of humanist critique and challenge. This is certainly the case if one monitors humanist's conversations and activities. So, theism is the problem.

Some might ask, what's the difference between theism and religion? At times there appears little distinction: theists consider themselves religious and in the United States the vast majority of those who understand themselves to be religious are theists. True, yet there is an important distinction to be made and the usefulness of this distinction enters humanist camps, for example, as the idea of *religious* humanism is brought into play. Mind you, adherents to this are often (if not typically) humanists who do not hold to supernatural claims, but in many cases attend to rituals—e.g., church services—that they consider religious. No God or gods. But, from their vantage point, they nonetheless are religious. This situation has created something of a tension felt in many humanist meetings and gatherings; yet, from my perspective this isn't a necessarily negative tension.

At this point, I want to make what I consider an important distinction that goes this way. Theism is the structuring of life around belief in cosmic forces and supernatural "realities." Religion, on the other hand, is simply by definition "a binding together." Religion can be thought of as a particular framing of and response to the fundamental and haunting questions of human existence: Who are we? What are we? Why are we? When are we? Where are we? Sure, science broadly conceived (and I include the social sciences and humanities here) wrestles with these in a manner pretended to be objective. Yet, there is a more emotional and subjective response as well to these questions and that takes the form of religion. So, in that it is an effort to render life meaningful, to develop a fuller sense of human subjectivity as conscious and self-aware creatures, religion isn't synonymous with theism. In doing this work, religion assumes no gods and requires no concern with superhuman worlds of wonder. Religion and theism are not the same thing. In fact, theism is a type of religious orientation, but it certainly isn't the only way to think about religion. In itself, as an effort to wrestle with questions of our being and knowing, religion can be very historically situated and bound. It need not pull adherents into supernatural framings of life; transhistorical thinking isn't a requirement of religion. So conceived—and there are ample examples of religion understood this way—it is merely a tool, a human tool for unpacking and exploring the workings of human life.

Again, theism is a particular way of unpacking and exploring human life, but it does so in a way that can divest human life of its "earthy" quality by arguing its "true" meaning is part of some cosmic and divine plan developed and orchestrated by God/gods. Pointing beyond history can remove from humans accountability and responsibility for their actions by making human will subject to cosmic forces. God/gods are given ultimate knowledge of and control over human history and its content. Humanism does well when it points out and critiques this problematic framing of human life as a critical failure of theism.

When it comes to so-called racial minorities in the United States, this thinking on theism (again often confused within religion) prompts questions like this one: why would African Americans, whose enslavement was justified by Christianity, embrace Christianity? The content of this sort of question comes in a variety of forms—depending on the context for and environment in which the question is asked. Yet, the core concern is the same: theism is destructive and racial minorities participate (unknowingly?) in their own degradation through their overwhelming embrace of theism.

Why is this the fallback assumption concerning racial minorities and theism? In asking this question I am not attempting to soften critique against the wrong perpetuated through the ethics of Christianity and justified by Christian theology, as well as that of other modes of theism. No. *This isn't to say that an embrace of theism is a good move; it isn't.* However, *don't ask this question regarding why racial minorities participate in theism without historical context.* Instead, learn something about these communities and the nature of their engagement with theism. In a word, humanists need a more developed and more nuanced understanding of how and why racial minorities participate in Christianity and other theistic traditions. Only this type of robust and historically sensitive awareness can position humanism to say and do anything useful regarding the intersections of theism and race. Only this lucid approach to theism and race will equip humanists to sound informed, rather than ignorant, when talking to racial minorities about racial minorities. And not sounding ignorant goes a long way in producing more useful conversations and sustainable activism.

Still, mindful of the above, there is something to the question that has importance, when it is based on a sense of the religious history tied to racial minority communities. *So, here goes, many remain at least loosely associated with theism because theism within their communities has a mixed record—composed of life-denying thought and activities but also representing effort to advance the well-being of people within the confines of the material world. That is to say, they stay within theistic communities such as churches because these theistic communities have expressed—albeit in clumsy and inconsistent ways— an effort to appreciate and advance their personhood over against racism and other modes of discrimination and injustice. They stay because theistic communities, again in insufficient ways we must note, have attempted to use their inadequate tools to respond to the racial madness of U.S. society—a society that endorsed the poor treatment of "black," "brown," "red," and "yellow" peoples.*

For instance, it is true that a significant percentage of the African American population in the United States is involved with Christianity and other modes of theism. For the full presence of African Americans in North America, theism has served as a major cultural device for individual and collective life. But, it's important to recognize that Christianity—let's highlight the numerically most significant form of theism—in African American communities has had more than one purpose.

Sure, it served (and continues to function) as justification for the status quo. We all know its role as a major buttress for slavery and continued racial discrimination. We are aware of the ways in which it has sanctioned consumerism premised on the comfort of ministers who take resource from their congregations and offer in exchange only rhetoric and "pie in the sky." Or, in exchange for extreme financial gain, they offer the "keys" from scripture that can be used to secure wealth and prosperity. We call this approach to ministry "prosperity preaching." However, we are quick to forget the ways in which African American Christianity also pushed against injustice and worked— granted in flawed ways—to produce a sense of identity and agency that contradicted dehumanization produced through racial injustice. Keep in mind figures such as Nat Turner (1800–1831), Denmark Vesey (1767–1822), Gabriel Prosser (1776–1800), Sojourner Truth (1797–1883), and Harriet Tubman (1822–1913), and a host of others, who found in the Christian faith a source of support for activism. Believers all, the first three found a demand for justice within theism and their allegiance to a cosmic force. This call for the liberation of the oppressed moved beyond the rhetoric and more passive approaches of some to a call for counterviolence (slavery being the first mode of violence). They were willing to shed blood in order to bring about the freedom of the enslaved. Gabriel Prosser, for instance, didn't read in the biblical text a call for otherworldly thinking and contentment with oppression; rather, scripture demanded liberative action. His revolt failed, but estimates suggest as many as 50,000 enslaved Africans were ready to fight for freedom had the revolt gone as planned.

Sure, in the turn from the eighteenth to the nineteenth century when Prosser sought to organize a revolt, the fight for rights was part of an international (and somewhat secular) ethos due to the French Revolution and other efforts toward democracy, but theism figured into Prosser's demand for justice. This was also the case for Turner and Vesey. Both believed God demanded sociopolitical change. Vesey had purchased his freedom, but was deeply aware of the plight of those still held in bondage—this, combined with his religious zeal, pushed him to do something. He saw in the Hebrew Bible, for instance, a demand for justice played out through the Children of Israel that had relevance for his particular historical moment. He bargained an approach to faith framed by the theological-ethical assumption God required the liberation of enslaved Africans just as God had demanded the freedom of the Israelites. Hence, theism did not pacify but rather provided a language of social transformation and a motivation for an ethical position calling for radical change. Large numbers were willing to follow him, but the plot was discovered.

Turner, as the others, believed God called him to a great work—the freeing of the oppressed. He saw in scripture all the necessary evidence to support violent revolt against the injustice of slavery. And, like the others already mentioned, the plot did not produce the desired change, but that isn't what's important here. The essential idea is less result driven and is simply a challenge to the assumption African Americans and other racial minorities should abandon theism because it has never supported reason, logic, and quality of life.

Why African Americans and others continue to participate in theistic communities has something to do with the type of tradition of rebellion suggested by figures like Turner, Vesey, and Prosser—not to mention the many unnamed enslaved (and free) Africans who used more passive means of rebellion (e.g., breaking tools to slowdown work and poisoning whites) and understood this work as consistent with—if not demanded by—their faith.

Black men weren't the only African Americans who understood the teachings of theism as consistent with demands for justice. A Methodist by religious inclination, Sojourner Truth was an advocate for the end of slavery and equal rights for women. Her "Ain't I a Woman" (1851) speech turned attention explicitly to the plight of black women who suffered from a double bind in the United States: they were black and they were women. Sojourner Truth wasn't her given name (Isabella Baumfree), but instead was the name she gave herself in 1843 in response to what she understood as a divine call to proclaim the truth and free those in bondage. Harriet Tubman took a different route. While securing her freedom like Truth by escape as opposed to "legal" emancipation, Tubman made it her mission to go back and lead others to freedom by means of the "underground railroad." She also helped rebel John Brown (1800–1859) secure participants for his attack on Harpers Ferry. These activities along with her service as a cook and nurse during the Civil War, and her campaign for women's rights, were motivated by her theistically fueled rejection of the slave system.

Outside theistically inspired rebellion, there are other ways in which—even humanists must acknowledge—the historical black church has attempted to address the demands of life in the material world.

Two Great Awakenings, the first in the eighteenth century and the second during the nineteenth century, brought large scores of European Americans and African Americans into Christian communities, with Baptists and Methodists gaining the bulk of those converts. People moved into these two denominations because these churches gave less attention to learning formal doctrines and creeds, and instead gave energetic priority to experiencing the presence of God through impassioned worship. Methodists and Baptists also gave ministerial opportunities to European Americans and African Americans without a prerequisite of formal training. So, there was some degree—limited as it was—of spiritual equality, or at least the recognition of shared spiritual interests. But what church involvement didn't promote was an end to sociopolitical and economic inequality.

In addition to participation in congregations run by others, African Americans also forged new denominations with stronger commitments to battling racism as a proper response to Christian commitment. The African Methodist Episcopal Church, various Baptist denominations, and a variety of other churches grew and made their mark, claiming many of the most significant leaders of African American communities. In addition, numerous scholars argue it is out of these early African American Christian communities one finds the development of theologized modalities of activism—all of which place at the center of thought a God committed to justice—to justice *above all else.*

Early examples of thinkers within this theistically inspired activism would have to include Henry McNeal Turner, a bishop within the African Methodist Episcopal Church who argued, "God is a Negro." He proclaimed this doctrine of God roughly a century before James Cone, the founder of academic black theology, proclaimed in 1969 the blackness of God. Maria Stewart, in 1831, became the first African American woman to lecture publically on political issues. She gave religious-theological attention to issues of gender in ways that would spark the interest of late-twentieth-century black women who outlined an approach to progressive theological reflection, drawing from figures such as Stewart and the work of Alice Walker, named womanist theology. This form of theology—along with black theology—is about the business of bringing theistic sensibilities to bare on issues of injustice, proclaiming all the time that proper conduct in the world is a demand of theistic commitment.

The story doesn't end with these various African American denominations and their leadership. To the contrary, when viewed without the assumption of Christianity as the only prevalent form of theism, history reveals the presence of a variety of theistic traditions active within the communities of racial minorities. For instance, at least 5 percent of the enslaved Africans brought to the Americas were Muslim, and there is compelling evidence suggesting at least some of these Muslims thrived in North America. African-based traditions anchored by West African deities also informed African American religious life, as did more stripped down versions such as hoodoo and conjure. Over the years, the list of traditions would grow to include the Nation of Islam, the Five Percent Nation, the Black Jews, Father Divine's Peace Mission, Sweet Daddy Grace's Universal House of Prayer for All Peoples, Voodoo, etc. Each one of these and others unnamed here claims the loyalty and devotion of African Americans across the country.

The arrangement and transmission of these various traditions are complex and deeply embedded in the cultural worlds of African Americans. They have been expressed through formal doctrine, creeds, and rituals. They have been informally and orally transmitted. And, they are represented by means of cultural production—such as quilts marked by theistic signs and symbols. Songs have expressed their theological insights. Poems have spoken to the depths of devotion. Styles of dress have portrayed the aesthetic of theism. And, plants as well as other natural items have been mined as storehouses of spiritual power.

The theistic landscape of African American communities is and has always been complex, rich, and layered with competing faith claims. In significant ways, many of these traditions are mutually dependent—borrowing doctrine and ritual structures, modifying others, and building on an explicit rejection of still others. Yet, even these points of strong disagreement demonstrate the manner in which African American religious history, hence, American religious history, involves explicit (and implicit) exchange between various faiths. Each speaks to a particular way to address the spiritual and mundane needs of life.

In some instances these traditions reject racist dehumanization through a robust celebration of blackness as a marker of divine selection and specialness. Regarding Christianity and the Nation of Islam, for instance, this special status involves a unique relationship between African Americans and divinity. With the former this entails a sense that God favors them, like the Children of Israel, and God will work on their behalf. For the latter, Elijah Muhammad taught that Allah created "the Blackman" as the "original man," from which all other people came, and the Blackman is the rightful ruler of the Universe. These are but two examples of the numerous ways in which African Americans have used religious faith to counter racist thought and practice.

It is also the case, jumping through the centuries, that many African Americans embraced (and continue to embrace) Christianity because of its cultural, social, and economic potentialities. That is to say, they aren't convinced by its theology but instead are pragmatic and see it as a resource for enhancing the secular dimensions of life—jobs, cultural connections, social networks, political power, and activism.

All that said, the relationship between African Americans and Christianity is complex and layered. And, more stinging in this regard, humanism and other human-centered philosophies and strategies didn't always support African American efforts toward social transformation through the end of racism and its systemic markers. Theists weren't the only ones to hold slaves. And, theists aren't the only ones who, historically, have downplayed the significance of racial justice by "blaming the victims" and positing African American collective misery is a consequence of African American failure to do better.

Theism's use as a tool of historical situation transformation isn't limited to African Americans in the United States, nor is it limited to

Christianity in a strict sense. Take into consideration the manner in which traditions such as Vodun (or what we have commonly called Voodoo) played a role in the Haitian Revolution. This tradition, which made its way to North America by means of the slave trade and ongoing migration, is premised on the assumed reality of forces—the *loa* constituting an expansive grouping of deities—moving through the world, impinging on human life. They work for and with devotees. They can be bargained with for the benefit of human well-being. When properly beseeched—e.g., through offerings and gifts—these *loa* provide energy, wisdom, power, etc., traits necessary for humans to impact others. Although Vodun represents a blending of Catholicism and West African cosmological tradition, it doesn't contain the sense of original sin, for instance, that plagues so many Christians and limits their appreciation for the human capacity for will and thereby profound activity.

The exact number of adherents to Voodoo/Vodun in the United States is uncertain, but its presence is as old as Christian communities and people in the twenty-first century continue to embrace it because it provides a steady, although imperfect, means by which to counter some of the effects of racial discrimination by advancing the potential for human action and importance.

Haiti isn't alone in providing theistic sensibilities that would make their way to the United States and influence the sensibilities of so-called racial minorities. Cosmic forces in Cuba also came to the aid of enslaved Africans. Combining Catholicism with West African practices and philosophies, a tradition we have called "Santeria" or the "African Way" served as a tool by means of which "Hispanics" sought to foster their well-being. The various deities that form the pantheon of divine beings interact with humans in a consistent manner, including through direct contact with human bodies. These forces, from the perspective of practitioners, are often personification of natural forces such as oceans, rivers, etc., and covered by catholic saints who were considered simply other manifestations of these African gods. They, in some way or another, aid humans in working through the materiality of their physical existence. No real talk of heaven or hell, but rather a deep regard for making the arrangements of material life as compelling and useful as possible. During the period of slavery, this tradition and others like it aided certain segments of the Cuban population to survive the dehumanizing circumstances shaping their lives. Their ritualized practices from the period of slavery moving forward served to provide opportunity for despised populations to recognize their value over against the destructive social circumstances in which they lived. With time—due to importation of enslaved Africans from the Caribbean as well as later migration patterns— this tradition gained a hold on certain regions of the United States. And so, participation within Santeria in what is called a "house" or *ile* speaks not only to some type of supernatural connection but also to cultural pride. Involvement in this tradition also entails recognition of a shared history, and a type of shared personhood, again, in contrast to the limited value attached to status as a so-called racial minority within a country, the United States, that has privileged whiteness.

Above I provide examples of ways in which theism(s) has been changed, adapted, and used to provide some space for racial minorities to feel more of their worth and value over against the politics of a racialized society. According to some scholars and activists, such a use of theism hasn't been possible for American Indian peoples whose cultural—e.g., family structure, political practices, social arrangements, sense of identity, and personal meaning—were damaged deeply by the imposition of Christianity. In this way, their perspective on Christianity is similar to that of many humanists. However, it doesn't end there. While condemning Christianity, many of these scholars and activists advocate the importance of traditional American Indian metaphysics and ritualization of life. Grounded in deep regard for and connection to the natural environment (offering careful attention to how we occupy space) and privileging concern with life balance, traditional thinking and practices served (and continue to serve some would argue) as a foil against colonial forces that marginalize and brutalize life. As with Voodoo and Santeria, there is here a connection to ancestors that grounds life and seeks to connect the individual to a larger and robust community of concern. All this speaks to the fundamental importance of relationship, mutuality, and synergistic arrangements of life, thought, and activity.

There is in American Indian traditions a push to join humans to other modalities of life in a web of respect and connection. In this regard, for many embracing traditional American Indian philosophies of life, the "we" is more important than the "I."

With all this talk of theism that isn't dismissive in a crude manner, it's important I provide some perspective—or, in other words, show my humanism "membership card."

Humanists are right to critique the supernatural claims of theistic traditions, but this challenge to belief must involve sensitivity to what participants understand as theism's material value—the manner in which it provides some reprieve from the brutal conditions of life in a racialized society. Theism isn't reasonable—but there is more to an embrace of theism than theological markers, signs, and symbols. Again, its complicated and humanist conversations should reflect recognition of this complexity.

Yes, racial minorities remain within organizations that have also destroyed life, perverted justice, and supported the status quo. But, what I'm suggesting, no, arguing here is the way in which allegiance to theism isn't simply about theology. Rather, it also has something to do with practice—the ways in which theistic communities historically have tried to buttress the life options of oppressed racial minorities against the onslaught of white supremacy. It is this commitment to any effort—as flawed and inconsistent as it is—that keeps many within theistic communities. What they offer is imperfect, but, it's something.

At the very least, these organizations "get it," which is to say they understand the absurd nature of life within a racialized society that devalues some communities based on superficial markers such as skin color. They sit in services or participate in other activities and don't have to explain themselves; don't have to justify their disappointment, annoyance, and anger over the ways in which the larger society belittles, mocks, and abuses them in so many ways. In the context of these deeply flawed theistic communities, no one ask the participates, "why are you people so angry?"

This isn't an endorsement of theism. (Of course, theism should go away.) Nor is it an effort to explain away their destructive dimensions and characteristics. Rather, it's context I'm offering here. It's an effort to explain why people stay, which isn't the same as embracing what these traditions believe.

What I've written here should spark another question, a more appropriate question for humanists. *Rather than asking why are so-called racial minorities still theists, ask this: why hasn't humanism proven a more compelling alternative to theism for African Americans, American Indians, Latinos/as, and so on?*

By asking this question, humanists avoid the assumption the problem is with racial minorities and instead rightly highlight the potential defect in the available options for them. It avoids any of the ignorant stereotypes that assume the emotional nature of racial minorities, which assumes their inability to grasp the intellectual rigor of humanism, and so on. Theism draws them away from logic and reason and supports a variety of problematic intellectual and sociopolitical positions. But, humanism hasn't attracted them in the numbers one might expect, even when one considers the growth in the number of "nones" and the clear troubles within theism.

There are ways in which humanism (outside associations such as the Unitarian Universalist Association) fails to recognize the need to ritualize life. That is to say, too often nontheists such as humanists assume that only theists need ritual—and that to entertain the development of humanist rituals is to open the door to theism.

While issues of policy are vital, to deny the importance of ritual is to overlook the human desire for meaning and the dimensions of ourselves that don't respond to rigid analysis. Connected to this conversation regarding ritual is the human desire for community, for connection to something greater than the individual. Theists often speak of this in terms of transcendence; but, that isn't the only way to address the nature of this yearning. For the humanist, it isn't supernatural. It has nothing to do with an effort to push beyond human history and its restrictions. Rather, it is simply a way to note the social dimensions of human existence—the individual within the context of the larger web of life. While humanists fight over the relevance of ritual and community, theistic organizations assume the importance of these two. And, many racial minorities will put up with the more offensive dimensions of theism and theistic gatherings for the sake of some sense of community (including opportunities for networking, for cultural connection, and for services). Putting up with what they theologically disagree with affords them some attention to the need to render life meaningful, and some way to ritualize all this so as to make important our occupation of time and space. Mindful of this, we might even expand the question above just a bit:

Why hasn't humanism proven a more compelling alternative to theism for African Americans, American Indians, Latinos/as, and so on? ***And, what might humanism do—on the level of community formation and the ritualizing of mundane life—to make it more appealing and more competitive with theistic organizations?***

* * *

If You Want to Know More

Many of the ideas above are drawn from or inspired by my earlier work and by books listed below. For readers who want more detail concerning the complexity of theism's ethics and activism, or want more information concerning the humanist challenge of community and ritual, the following short list of materials will prove useful.

Brandon, George. *Santeria from Africa to the New World* (Bloomington, IN: Indiana University Press, 1993).

Deloria, Vine. *Custer Died for Your Sins: An Indian Manifesto* (Norman, OK: University of Oklahoma Press, 1969).

Du Bois, W. E. B. *The Souls of Black Folk* (New York: Penguin Classics, 1996).

Espinosa, Gaston and Mario T. Garcia, editors. *Mexican American Religions: Spirituality, Activism, and Culture* (Durham, NC: Duke University Press, 2008).

Floyd-Thomas, Stacey M. and Anthony B. Pinn, editors. *Liberation Theologies in the United States: An Introduction* (New York: New York University Press, 2010).

Malcolm X, *The Autobiography of Malcolm X* (New York: Ballantine Books, 1992).

Nakanishi, Don T. and James S. Lai, editors. *Asian American Politics: Law Participation and Policy* (Boulder, CO: Rowman and Littlefield, 2003).

Olson, James S. *Equality Deferred: Race, Ethnicity, and Immigration in American Since 1945* (Belmont, CA: Thomson Wadsworth, 2003).

Pinn, Anthony B. *Humanism: Essays on Race, Religion, and Popular Culture* (London: Bloomsbury, 2015).

Roman, Reinaldo L. *Governing Spirits: Religion, Miracles, and Spectacles in Cuba and Puerto Rico, 1898-1956* (Chapel Hill, University of North Carolina Press, 2007).

Talbot, Steve, *Roots of Oppression: The American Indian Question* (New York: International, 1981).

Takakai, Ronald. *A Different Mirror: A History of Multicultural America* (New York: Little, Brown and Company, 1993).

Wilmore, Gayraud S. *Black Religion and Black Radicalism: An Interpretation of the Religious History of African Americans* (Maryknoll, NY: Orbis Books, 2003).

2

POOR RACIAL THINKING AND POOR BEHAVIOR

Humanism is driven by reason and logic, and so it doesn't see race as a biological reality that should determine any significant dimension of life.

* * *

While it is true, as we know, some Europeans who ventured to North America came with theistic beliefs in tow. And, they used these beliefs as one way (out of many) to frame the parameters of community and to forge a shared vocabulary and grammar of life. However, this is not to say the United States—the "Nation" —was founded as a Christian nation. It wasn't. We know this all too well!

It was founded as an economic opportunity occasioned by technological advances that made possible the shrinking of the globe, the expansion of empire beyond the "old world" models of monarchy, and the communication of success and happiness as not confined in a strict sense to social standing but rather to hard work. In short, the United States is premised on a new narrative of opportunity, independence, tenacity, and special status. True, some of the rhetoric for this narrative is drawn from theological vocabulary and grammar. But even this language typically is devoid of the metaphysical assumptions that guide the traditions from which this way of communicating is drawn.

The privileged class that developed the founding documents of the United States was in large part suspicious of Roman Catholicism, assuming allegiance to the Pope would no doubt hamper allegiance to the Nation. And, there were significant conflicts between various Protestant communities, which meant a somewhat limited ability to spread the teachings of these traditions. The Two Great Awakenings (mentioned in chapter one) marked a significant increase in certain traditions—Baptist and Methodist for the most part—but this still left large segments of the growing North American experiment untouched by the energetic embrace of theism. The indigenous population held to its own belief structures, and African-based traditions, along with Islam, had a hold—albeit not necessarily numerically significant—on segments of the population of enslaved (and free) African Americans. It is safe to say theism was a volatile arrangement in the United States— composed of competing (often violently so) faith stances. Added to this mix was an important community of nontheists (e.g., skeptics, humanists, atheists, and freethinkers)—many of whom played key roles in the mapping out of the sociopolitical and economic structure of the new nation.

What undergirded these disparate communities of faith and disbelief was a fairly common perception of race. A rather consistent theory of race premised on the dominance of European lineage marked a common narrative of the United States. Philosopher Cornel West has done a brilliant job of mapping out what he calls the "genealogy of race" that informs the Modern West—i.e., the Age of Exploration through the Industrial Revolution and the Second World War. According to West, the Modern World is premised on a connection between the "look" of bodies and the structure of "civilization." In a word, populations were divided by racial look and this look was used to determine the value and importance of particular peoples. The Greek body type (as displayed in early art) was understood as the ideal body form and those closest to this ideal where considered more beautiful, intelligent, more capable, and of greater value. Those further from the Greek body type were considered of less importance, less beautiful, less intelligent, less capable, and *suited for service to Europeans* (i.e., those closest to the ideal body type).

Racial difference wasn't always tied to larger issues of basic value and cultural importance. For instance, European records of initial contact between Europeans and Africans note their difference in look. This difference is addressed as a curiosity—a superficial distinction that is without larger and lasting consequences. However, the growth of economic opportunity in the Americas prompted greater need for labor that couldn't be met by indentured European servants or the coerced labor of American Indians. Africans, however, fit the bill in that the climate wouldn't be a major challenge; they had agricultural skills, and the population was plentiful. Yet, making use of this new labor pool in growing and more violent manners required justification. Racial difference as marking more substantive differences in intellect, value, and importance made the atrocities of enslavement easier to digest. In essence, the argument went this way. Africans don't have the same capacities, the same intrinsic value, and this is verified by the fact that they don't look like (and don't live like) Europeans. Furthermore, their assumed lack of acquaintance with Christianity was used as confirmation of their inferiority. (The fact that the Ethiopian Coptic Church is an ancient church, and that Christianity had already spread across the continent of African from East to West, wasn't a consideration.) The Bible was used to justify this perception, particularly the story of Ham in which the son of Ham—Canaan—is cursed (Genesis 9:20–27). As a condition of this curse his descendants (assumed to be Africans) were to be servants for the rest of time. The Bible provided a particular metaphysical justification but over time science (the "pseudo-sciences") would be used to provide what was considered an objective justification for this racial categorization and demand for perpetual servitude. Consistent with popular thinking, the manner in which enslaved Africans were sold at auction, along with livestock, spoke to the assumption they weren't fully human. And, descriptions of enslaved Africans highlighted what Europeans considered their odd—if not bizarre—and exaggerated features. This "look" made them acceptable not for full citizenship but for full labor.

Both advocates for slavery and those opposed to it tended to assume the inferiority of Africans. Some abolitionists, for instance, opposed the enslavement of Africans on theological grounds, but this didn't mean they understood enslaved Africans as being of full and equal status to whites. They, Africans, were human but of a less significant kind. It was this basic humanity that required freedom, but it wasn't a human status sufficient to also necessitate full citizenship and socioeconomic and political equality. Social ramifications of this assumed inferiority continued over the centuries—displayed in popular culture, anticipated in all interactions, and reenforced through the political arrangements of public life. And so, exaggerated depictions of African Americans were used to sell a variety of products and to provide social comfort for whites, who might be poor or in other ways marginalized—still at least they weren't black. But, more importantly these stereotypical presentations served to justify harsh treatment and limited opportunity for people of African descent.

Of course strides were made to change this situation, to adjust the place of African Americans in the collective life of the Nation—the Emancipation Proclamation, Civil Rights legislations, and so on. On the theoretical level, some of the rigor or sting of racial classification and injustice has been attacked at the root by arguing, correctly so, that race is a social construction. There is nothing biological about it, nothing actually verifiable or substantiated through actual scientific investigation. Rather, it is a cultural category, a matter of language and public conversation with no roots in the inherent constitution of the human. Put another way, race is what we communicate (or say) about each other and not what we are in actuality. It is a lens used to view humans and as such it has no necessary importance. By extension, it shouldn't serve as a reality that authorizes disregard, disrespect, or injustice.

A matter of human imagination, it should have no unbreakable hold on human life, although it often has had this type of power. We have clear markers of this. Religious traditions and other metaphysics serve to justify at times the maintenance of racial categories as marking divinely willed difference with strong connotations and consequences. Within old texts such as the Bible, negative color symbolism portrays "black" as representing "evil," or otherwise being a strong sign of a problem, and white serves as a symbol of "purity." This negative color symbolism is projected unto bodies in a manner that can't be tested in a lab. Quite simply, "God wants it this way."

Grounded in supernatural claims and "feelings," there are limited ways to challenge this theological assumption that shapes and confines attitudes toward African Americans. Sure, there's nothing empirical about the claim of divine sanction for racialization of human communities. Nonetheless, those who make this argument read any event or conversation to their theological advantage. That, indeed, is the nature of theological discourse and its consequences: it's plastic in nature, flexible—a type of linguistic virus that takes advantage of its host. Furthermore, negative consequences of race have their genius in the manner in which racial discourse takes place without our having to consciously acknowledge it. Think about it: as early sociologist and historian W. E. B. Du Bois noted in 1903, the twentieth century is marked by the "color line." In fact, it is defined by the shape, tone, and texture of racial categorizations and their felt implications. He saw no dimension of life immune to this situation—a context in which African Americans and other racial minorities serve as a problem to solve as opposed to being portrayed as vital and vibrant participants in the public workings of the nation.

Problematic notions of race that undergird racism as played out in politics, economics, social arrangements, and so on are a matter of "gut knowledge," as some scholars have put it. By that these scholars mean race/racism is played out not only through what we say, but also through all the other senses: we smell race, feel race, taste race, see race, hear race. And, nothing about participation in this process requires formal, book knowledge or study. For example, we assume certain foods are associated with certain racial groups: think about the jokes concerning fried chicken and watermelon. We assume certain words, or certain ways of speaking and sounding, are associated with particular racial groups. We assume particular smells are associated with particular racial (and class) groups. So much of this is worked through unconsciously because the codes associated with race classification and racial bias are ingrained in us through socialization.

Some of the more graphic depictions of race and racism in the United States are easily drawn from the teachings and practices of theistic organizations. And, humanists take great pride in distinguishing themselves from these theists, who give empirical value to bad "ideas" of race. The assumption here is that commitment to reason and logic, to empirical and material considerations, accompanied by a deep appreciation for the parameters of history, distinguish humanists from their poor thinking and bad behaving theist co-citizens. As a consequence, for some humanists, issues of racial justice and other attacks on problematic social constructs isn't proper humanist business. Race, because it isn't scientific and isn't reasonable, doesn't merit a great deal of attention. Rather, the argument goes, humanists should concern themselves with dismantling theism's assumed grip on the United States through attention to separation of church and state as well as science education. For these humanists—often a somewhat vocal group—justice issues are a distraction and not the proper business of humanist organizations because humanism, they assume, by its very nature, doesn't contribute to the maintenance of social injustice.

Many humanists are keen to argue the very documents that mark out the democratic nature of this nation speak to humanist sensibilities and concerns by lodging human life in the material world and to notions of fulfillment and happiness that aren't grounded in the will of some unseen force or forces. It isn't God's will that marks the parameters of the good life. Instead, it is adherence to the rights and opportunities forged through human law that marks out the path to success. "Life, liberty, and the pursuit of happiness" becomes the standard and religion is tolerated to the extent it has little to say to or about this secular quest for life balance. That is, government won't mess with religious institutions and religious institutions have no governmental control. Life isn't guaranteed by some cosmic something. No, humans have freedom and insight necessary to achieve for themselves a quality of existence that isn't discussed in terms of a desire to secure heaven but is real and materially situated. Human laws outlined by reasonable people (typically gender dynamics have reduced this to men) rather than divine regulations drawn from "sacred" texts guide life and measure outcomes.

In short, the United States is based on rugged thought and it comes to a head within the founding documents that outline the character and sensibilities of the nation. The USA isn't a monarchy led by priests and personalities; but rather a (limited) democracy premised on the participation of the populace, all framed by the texture and contours of human history. As figures such as Thomas Paine made clear, this political situation isn't the total destruction of religion but rather the separation of religion and politics—safeguarding each: politics as a public language of collective life, and religion as a private position suitable only for private life. Still Paine encouraged the religious to interrogate their faith, to analyze their faith through reason and in this way acknowledge its shortcomings and the areas of life unsuitable for it.

Besides Paine's push for life within the confines of reason, humanists are quick to speak the name of Thomas Jefferson as another amongst their numbers. Yes, take Jefferson for example. I've not encountered (and of course this is quite a limited survey) many who exclude him from their list of standout humanists who represent the best antitheism thinking. After all, he articulated much of the language that shaped the political infrastructure of the United States, and in addition he was a major advocate for higher education. These are just some of Jefferson's accomplishments. Mindful of his work, there is good reason for humanists to champion Jefferson and other high-profile figures understood as humanistic in orientation. Why wouldn't humanists do this, when the United States remains decidedly suspicious of nontheists? Isn't it a way of striking back at those who speak ill of humanism?

Remarking that they wouldn't vote for an atheist, is just one of the ways in which nontheism is demonized. Levels of perceived trustworthiness are also linked directly in the popular imagination of the United States to belief in the Divine. On the personal level, it isn't unheard of for those who are openly nontheistic to lose family, friends, employment, and other connections because of their vocal disbelief. Narratives of this disregard and neglect are numerous; they pepper formal presentations, lectures, and books as well as more informal conversations within humanist circles.

Suffice it to say, it isn't easy being a vocal and visible nontheist in the United States. Theists claim all that is good and all that is promising, and blame nontheists for all that is tragic. From natural disasters to human violence, theists are quick to point the finger at nonbelievers: God is punishing the United States of America, the story goes, for the disbelief of some. Through this misery, by means of a pedagogy of tragedy, God is proving both God's existence and displeasure. In this way, theists both pray for and prey on humanists—the irreligious scapegoat bound for hell.

What humanist isn't aware of this situation, and on some level impacted by it? I'm not breaking ground with this rehearsal of hatred against nonbelievers. One doesn't have to watch Fox News in order to get a sense of how despised are humanists and their way of being. How many small or large gatherings of humanists don't include some attention to personal narratives and group experiences of theist-bias? These and similar arrangements constitute humanist therapy of a sort, a sense of commonality—a shared plight that links humanists against the illogical and irrational in the world. Such an effort to develop a cushion against theist hate, I would suggest, is meant to assert the importance of the despised through a counter denouncement: Humanists aren't the problem; in fact, humanism is deeply embedded in the documents that ground this democracy experiment we call the United States. So, rather than disbelief as the source of U.S. troubles, theism is positioned by humanists as a virus of sorts—one that can be managed and treated through logic and reason.

Theism is the fundamental problem destroying not only the United States but also the world more generally. Radical Islam and fundamentalist Christianity are given as two popular examples of theologies that encourage if not demand destructive behavior and that position such violence (e.g., terrorist attacks and attacks on healthcare providers) as the stuff of righteousness and the work necessary in order to secure spiritual well-being and eternal reward. God demands it, or so they say, but there is no way to verify this and they don't seek proof beyond scripture, outside a gut feeling of assurance. For them, destruction is both the cause and the proof of divine presence, and only—the "logic" goes—those blinded by sin and spiritual perversion don't see it. As they say, the "fool" proclaims there is no God. Damn (in more than one way)! Others—such as

Buddhism and Hinduism—are not thought of as being as dangerous, or threatening in the same manner. They are perceived as delusional and premised on counterproductive approaches to life.

Both sides sling rhetorical bombs—but the theists with more ammunition and with bigger outlets. When outgunned, so to speak, humanists have attempted to match numbers with greater energy and strategic aggression. As it goes without saying, this is a stressful situation for nontheists—calling home a country within which a significant percentage of the population understands you as unprincipled, depraved, immoral, and untrustworthy. But we humanists haven't taken this without fighting back. Billboards, lawsuits, podcasts, television appearances, and public critique and celebration of humanism are some of the ways in which humanism's value has been mapped out. This alone, however, doesn't speak to the manner in which humanism is integral to the nation—part of its very foundation. Again, naming the great United States citizens who were within the humanist camp has served to tie this way of thinking and living to what it means to be "American." Tying the formation and ongoing workings of the United States to humanism is a good move—strategic, really, in a variety of ways.

My point here isn't to simply rehearse what humanists already know about theism, or what they know about their own response to theism. This information is just context for a more important conversation embedded within humanist challenges to theism and celebration of humanism's positive impact on the democratic way of life in the United States. In short, it isn't what humanists say (about themselves or theist opponents) but rather what isn't said that marks the difficulty not always acknowledged in a meaningful way, or rarely in ways that inform the "look" of humanist organizations and the nature of organizational policies and strategies. Put in different words, celebration of humanists across the centuries often fails to acknowledge the underbelly of humanism, or the ways in which it is similar to theism: both have a long legacy of problematic stances toward race.

According to Susan Jacoby, only two freethinkers, or humanists, have received appropriate attention—Thomas Jefferson and James

Madison. I am not in a position to advance nor deny that argument. And for the purposes of this text such an exploration isn't necessary. Suffice it to say, they are important figures within the history of the United States and within humanist circles. And, the relationship between freethought and race presented by such figures is instructive. Both were men of great intellect and profound importance for the establishment of the United States as a secular nation, and both at least passively endorsed (e.g., inherited slave estates) the system of slavery.

What I offer here isn't a history lesson on the philosophy of these two figures, but rather something about them and humanists' appreciation for them speaks to challenges regarding race worthy of addressing. I'm not especially concerned with the details of their secular thinking, the degrees to which they were definable as humanists based on contemporary understandings of the terminology. The fact that humanists claim them and do so with significant energy, for my purposes, is sufficient. They, as some might put it, are case studies of a sort that point to some incorrect assumptions made by some humanists. Secular government was and remained intimately linked to the problem of race acted out as racism. What are contemporary humanists to say about this?

For instance, again take Thomas Jefferson and his undeniable importance with respect to the articulation of the principles, values, and ideals that shape democracy in the United States, as well as his significance regarding public, higher education vis-à-vis the University of Virginia. Jefferson was also a slaveholder, whose wealth and influence was dependent upon a system of brutality that held in inhumane bondage peoples of African descent—beings whose humanity was questioned and who were without will to determine their own life options. He framed the workings of democracy as the political system of the new United States, but he supported the system of slavery through his direct participation in it. I've not heard much made of this latter point. Yet, isn't it important? Doesn't it provide a warrant for humility, and for a more balanced presentation of humanism, warts and all?

Theists assume the plausibility of perfection and as a consequence demand its significant figures be without flaws or at least—like the biblical figure King David—have notable signs of God's favor that blur out the messiness of life or at least point beyond it. Paradox and tension are difficult for theists, certainly when the paradox isn't resolved or the tension eased. For theists, history is purpose driven; the universe is concerned with and about humanity. And, situations and topics that challenge the pleasantries of this assumption trouble theists. On the other hand, humanists, with a more mature sense of humanity, shouldn't hold to the same demand for a stain-free existence. But yet, there appears to be at least a passive effort to remove the taint of racism from humanist legends such as Jefferson. Yes, Jefferson feared slavery would destroy the nation in that it was a plague with dire consequences. He believed ending slavery in Virginia and elsewhere also held the potential to flood the nation with a population it could not absorb and that couldn't integrate in a significant manner because of its inherent and undeniable inferiority.

Here we have it in brief: a significant humanist figure with significance to the United States from its initial formation to the present is also a prime example of the status quo in the form of race-based oppression. In a word, Jefferson represents both humanism and racism. One might argue Jefferson and those like him were "men" of their age—trapped in the workings of their time period and shaped by the sociocultural codes of that historical moment. This is true and this is why I would never suggest we ignore, for instance, Jefferson's contributions to our particular structuring of democracy and our resulting best practices of collective life. However, recognizing this doesn't free humanists from also recognizing the manner in which he represents some of the most troubling practices of race-based violence witnessed in the modern period. The former is to be celebrated and the latter acknowledged with every effort to learn from bad policy and behavior, and not repeat it. Will such an admission—despite the fact that plenty of Christians bought and traded in slaves, disregarded American Indians, and abused Latinos/as—fuel hostility toward humanists and prove for the general U.S. population that humanism is immortal and flawed? Can humanists acknowledge participation in racism and maintain their critique of theistically fueled injustice?

It's a delicate balance to be sure: a problem *and* solution wrapped in one and tied together nicely with a bow of energetic prophecy that screams accept these proclamations or experience eternal damnation . . . because God loves you to death. Within Christianity, the dominant tradition in the United States, this tension is in part a consequence of a really low opinion of humans and human nature. Based on a rather bizarre creation story, humans start out behind the curve, with a warped nature—the stories go—marked by a tendency toward immorality, disobedience, and questionable values. Left to their own devices, this demented story continues, humans will do no good. And so Christians spend so much time trying to correct for this original flaw, while also thinking of their condition as an opportunity for God to prove God's goodness.

Those who are despised take every opportunity to demonstrate that actually they are beyond reproach—upstanding people, with integrity, values, and an important role to play in the life of the nation. A type of respectability guides this thinking: if we can prove ourselves acceptable—whatever that means at the time—we will gain the status and the position we merit. As I see it, some version of that thinking is in play in many humanist circles concerning a variety of topics. Still, to claim figures such as Thomas Jefferson and in this way lodge humanism in the workings of the United States is also to tie humanism to various modalities of racial injustice. What to do?

Humanists embrace this respectability position with issues such as racism; and, racial minorities such as African Americans have been forced to do it with respect to virtually every social ill. Any crime implicates all; any social slip implicates all, and so on. Will theists use this information (as well known as it is) against humanists? And, would such a strategy harm the effort of humanists to make the United States a more secular nation? And so there is in some quarters a tendency to hide the unpleasant dimensions of life lived by some humanists, to downplay any significance. This is an understandable approach, but it does raise a point worth consideration.

Still, to embrace Jefferson, then, is to acknowledge at least a subtle connection to both a legacy of profound humanist thought and a legacy of profound humanist racism. This does not mean humanism and humanists are inherently racist; but it does do damage to a too popular assumption that humanism doesn't bend to the social construction of race in ways that would make it a significant part of the racism problem.

This is all to say the question why are African Americans still Christian betrays a lack of historical nuance. It makes a problematic assumption concerning humanism. I mention it above, but let me say it again for effect: humanists have participated in the perpetuation of racism. Some humanists assume their dependency on science, reason, and logic prevents them from buying into or perpetuating social constructions of injustice. I venture to guess they believe this, again, because social injustice is illogical, and not grounded in reason or science. Still, we live in cultural worlds and even the most strident humanist is influenced and informed by these cultural worlds, which include structures of bias and prejudice.

Humanists can be racially uninformed, insensitive . . . even racist. Reason and logic didn't protect pillars of the nation such as Thomas Jefferson from racial injustice. Social codes and cultural normative structures of collective behavior are tenacious and so ingrained in U.S. society that they go without saying . . . and this is in part their power. There are ways in which it becomes easy to lose sight, to become oblivious to the manner in which participation in U.S. racialization is just so easy and so quiet.

Does this mean humanists are racist? That's a question of privilege and the power to enforce privilege in ways that hamper life options for the targeted group, and answering it is a bigger conversation that this short chapter can engage. But, sure, yes, some might very well be racist and others are just deeply misinformed. This larger issue—are humanists racist?—is certainly worth conversation, but for now it's simply important to recognize humanists can knowingly and unknowingly support racial injustice through the assumption humanism puts them beyond the realm of such illogical thinking and behaving. What I suggest is a bit of humility and perspective— recognition of the ways in which one can both fight and contribute to injustice.

What can humanists do to lessen racial injustice both inside and outside the "movement"?

For those committed to issues of racial justice, I understand the passion and energy brought to such work. However, keep in mind those who suffer most from these circumstances are best positioned to lead. So, ask what you can do to be of assistance, and then do it. Don't assume you get to give the "marching orders." Instead, be content with a supporting role—a role based on solidarity. White humanists, for example, don't get to determine what are appropriate markers of progress for racial minorities. Promote solidarity, and play the role assigned by those who are most directly and deeply impacted by issues of race and racism. This approach recognizes that those who are most familiar with a particular structure of injustice are best positioned to suggest how to address it and what are acceptable benchmarks of progress. Leave behind the missionary impulse, connect with progressive organizations and meaningful projects, and simply follow instructions—with critical thinking intact. What I mean to say by this remark is that in terms of racial justice, those most deeply impacted by racial discrimination get to suggest the agenda, and the strategies related to that agenda are worked out, then, in conversation with all committed to justice and in light of their expertise and skill set.

This doesn't mean surrendering critical thinking; it doesn't mean giving up the ability to ask questions and probe—to push. What it does mean, however, is recognizing differing levels of impact—different ways in which race/racism plays out. In other words, I am suggesting race/racism necessitates learning, studying, and acting in ways that acknowledge the structures of privilege in the United States. Some discomfort is part of the process in that racial justice involves awareness and correction of privilege. Humanists, I imagine, are more than willing to follow the lead of trained scientists on issues related to the material structure of life, and they do so without feeling as if they surrender critical thinking and the right to ask questions. On race, I'm suggesting a similar intellectual and social posture. My call isn't for humanists to give up "freethinking." Rather, I propose freethinking on the issues of race/racism should involve recognition that some encounter racism more directly than others, and that solidarity on issues of race/racism may entail thinking about racial progress from the vantage point of those outside one's own community of concern.

* * *

If You Want to Know More

Here are some texts that provide a bit more detail concerning some of the ideas expressed in this chapter. They provide additional context and offer a rich sense of some of the major concerns expressed in the discussion.

Hartman, Saidiya. *Scenes of Subjection: Terror, Slavery, and Self-Making in the Nineteenth-Century America* (New York: Oxford University Press, 1997).

Harvey, Paul. *Freedom's Coming: Religious Culture and the Shaping of the South from Civil War through the Civil Rights Era* (Chapel Hill, NC: University of North Carolina Press, 2005).

Hutchinson, Sikivu. *Moral Combat: Black Atheists, Gender Politics and the Values Wars* (Los Angeles: Infidel Books, 2011).

Jacoby, Susan. *Freethinkers: A History of American Secularism* (New York: Holt Paperbacks, 2005).

Marable, Manning. *The Great Wells of Democracy: The Meaning of Race in American Life* (New York: Basic Books, 2003).

Miller, John Chester. *Wolf by the Ears: Thomas Jefferson and Slavery* (Charlottesville, VA: University of Virginia Press, 1991).

Riley, Padraig. *Slavery and the Democratic Conscience: Political Life in Jeffersonian America* (Philadelphia: University of Pennsylvania Press, 2015).

Waldstreicher, David. *Slavery's Constitution: From Revolution to Ratification* (New York: Hill and Wang, 2010).

Winant, Howard. *The World Is a Ghetto: Race and Democracy Since World War II* (New York: Basic Books, 2002).

3

RACIAL MINORITIES AND HUMANISM

Humanism would be of great benefit to your community, wouldn't it? If only we could get more of you involved.

* * *

This isn't the exact phrasing of the question. I've actually heard it broached in a variety of ways. Often the target is theism still very present within African American and other racial minority communities. But at other times there is a more strongly expressed assumption that humanism is fairly new to racial minorities, that it has a long history within white communities, but not so long within other communities in the United States. At worst, the rationale offered for this is blatantly offensive: humanism is highly intellectual and without emotionalism. The underlying statement being made is simple: humanism is for intelligent and reasonable people, while "your" people tend to be more emotional. Such sentiments stem back to assumptions of racial minorities as childlike, or aggressive, or lacking intellectual ability and maturity. Often cast as a matter of environment or inherent qualities (or lack thereof), the consequence is the same: racial minorities aren't prominent in humanist circles at least in part because they are new arrivals to this very reasonable philosophy of life. One finds this thinking expressed both implicitly and explicitly within humanist circles. Yet, it couldn't be more wrong, more misguided, and more in need of correction. In short, humanism is an open philosophy of life and its organizational structure by and large is at least theoretically open to all who embrace particular definitions of humanism. However, the ability of humanists groups to maximize this openness in ways that mirror the high potential of diversity and inclusion requires some corrections to poor thinking, such as misconceptions concerning who is found when and where in the history of humanism.

Within the American Indian context, it is often asserted that philosophies of life entail humanist principles, including human accountability and responsibility for human conduct as well as a variety of other values grounded in the realities of the material world. While not necessarily named such, this type of earthly thinking and acting holds more in common with contemporary conceptions of humanism than it does contemporary conceptions of theism. Still, this shifting or blurred language doesn't provide grounding for assumptions that humanism belongs with those of European descent and has been borrowed recently by others. Humanism has a substantial and noteworthy—although underappreciated—presence beyond European-centered communities. When, for instance, one thinks about the Americas more broadly, figures such as Simón Bolívar, a freethinker, can't be forgotten for his role in the founding of Latin American states such as Venezuela and Ecuador. Or, one might think about José Marti—the historically significant Cuban thinker, writer, and political commentator—whose travels to North America spawned *Our America*, which framed an important interrogation of the nature and meaning of American identity (tied to the American Indian cultural presence as point of genesis). This work is often framed by some scholars, despite its flaws and shortcomings on particular issues, as having offered a "New American Humanism," by means of which Marti provided something with more than hints of naturalism as a proper framing for an "authentic" American self-understanding and public identity. He, as many scholars have noted, wanted to dismantle racial hierarchies through an appeal to a type of universal identity that undercuts such problematic notions of difference. This universal connection grounds the type of humanism he offers.

These are but a few examples of a history of humanism beyond white Americans that extends back well beyond the recent signposts of racial minority "Nones" who leave theism for the "safe haven" of humanism. If nothing else, these examples provide a reasoning to probe and poke holes in arguments that place racial minorities only uncomfortably in the recent history of American humanism. Still, perhaps the most systematically recorded challenge to this thinking about racial minorities as late arrivals to the humanist party involves the many articles and books written on African American humanism from the colonial period to the present.

Conversation may be dominated by attention to African Americans and deep theistic commitment—churches, mosques and so on. And, true, the landscape of African American communities is littered with monuments to theism. But, why assume this strong attention to theism means no equally robust concern for humanism? African Americans have been doing humanism for a very long time, for as long as there has been a nation in which to do it.

Again, for effect, I restate the basic idea: beyond the popular perception of African Americans as inherently theistic and historically Christian, there is an undercurrent of disbelief expressed in a variety of ways—songs, stories, narratives, autobiographies, and so on. For instance, many are familiar with the spirituals—those early songs by enslaved and free Africans by means of which they offered a theological take on their surroundings and life circumstances. We cannot accurately date the start of those theistic songs, but some experts suggest they are as old as the African presence in North America and involve a poetic merger of their religious sensibilities, artistic abilities, and the realities of their surroundings.

The exact dating of these songs isn't important here; rather, what is important is the fact that they were matched by songs—e.g., work songs and early modes of what we've come to call the blues—with a more naturalistic and a less supernatural inclination. These work songs and blues tunes rejected the theological assumptions of the spirituals and instead highlighted human accountability and responsibility, and framed all of this in terms of the material world and what can be known empirically. In a sense, these songs—forged before the 1776 demand for independence—mark out a rudimentary humanist ethos by critiquing and dismissing theistic arguments regarding life in favor of something more earthbound. The songs speak of hard work, racial injustice, hypocrisy, the desire for change, and they do so without any appeal to supernatural assistance.

Furthermore, African American folk wisdom and narratives match the nonsupernatural stance of the blues. These tales, collected in a variety of books, project a take on life that belittles superstition and highlights the need for African Americans to rely on themselves, not gods, and to use human ingenuity and creativity to counter racial injustice.

African Americans had to exercise caution within their music and their stories. Every effort had to be made not to alarm whites because they could easily exercise violence against African Americans without penalty. While this concern had to be acknowledged there was a desire—no need—to present a take on life that ran contrary to the status quo and the demands of white supremacy. That is to say, they had to outsmart whites, which was made all the easier due to assumptions that enslaved and free African Americans were childlike, less fully formed humans. They could smile and in this way pacify whites and still plot and plan for freedom.

So they sang songs with double meanings: one for and understood by African Americans, and the other with less threatening commentary for the benefit of white listeners. Work songs and other more secular modes of musical expression pushed a wisdom centered on human bodies and what they forge in the world. There is no unfounded optimism, but rather realism—a sense of doing what one can with what one has at one's disposal. There are no cosmic promises of justice elsewhere outside human history; but instead these songs present a sense that life is full of unresolved tension and paradox. And, we make our way through the world as we can always aware of our circumstances without being consumed by those circumstances.

This is a sentiment that moves throughout the history of humanistic thought and ethics. For example, the French North African philosopher Albert Camus centuries later would present a similar take on life when reflecting on the predicament of Sisyphus:

"One," Camus reflects, "must imagine Sisyphus happy"—not out of his condition but also not defeated by it. African Americans, as their humanist posture toward the world suggests, knew something of this moralist position. The musical tradition briefly noted above places both joy and pain in the material world, with attention to the ache of muscles and the confusion of minds without appeal to "spirit" or "soul." Scholars like Sterling Brown have made available lyrics such as these that speak to the posture toward the world I have in mind:

> Our father, who is in heaven,
> White man owe me eleven and pay me seven,
> Thy kingdom come, thy will be done,
> And if I hadn't took that, I wouldn't had none.

This reworking of the "Lord's Prayer" is a powerful juxtaposition to the traditional words to that prayer. Instead of surrendering to the will of some unknowable force, the song turns attention to the plight of labor in the world. Or, think in terms of this one: "I don't want to ride no golden chariot; I don't want no golden crown; I want to stay down here and be, just as I am without one plea." Readers who know something about spirituals and other religious tunes will understand the significance of the mocking tone that belittles spirituals that typically dismiss conditions in the material world in favor of promised heavenly rewards.

Many blues songs and blues performers chronicle, celebrate, and lament the stuff of physical assistance with little more than derision for those of a more spiritual inclination. At times blues figures such as Robert Johnson signify theism by turning "good" and "evil" on their heads, celebrating in the process what most theists within African American communities reject (e.g., drinking, gambling, premarital sex) and rejecting what they embrace (e.g., piety). It is dismissing by means of belittling the fundamental theological workings of, say, African American Christianity. At other times, these artists challenge theism through attention to marginal traditions such as conjure and hoodoo. Along these lines, even when theism is embraced, traditions such as conjure are noted for their ability to enhance human life within the confines of human history—to secure love, wealth, social standing, and so on—having no real regard for the typical trappings of theism such as heaven and the like. Typical religious imagery and signs—such as the number "7," considered the number of perfection—are turned on their head and made to highlight human prowess. Long after the initial development of the blues, Muddy Waters and Willie Dixon would give this turn to marginal traditions sentimental meaning. For instance, Muddy Waters claims significance in that he was born on the "seventh day," and his stature is clear: "Y'know I'm here; Everybody knows I'm here; And I'm the hoochie-coochie man; Everybody knows I'm here."

Theists in African American communities (and others as well) frown upon the pleasures of the flesh and refuse to measure human possibilities in light of what is empirically verifiable. But, the blues don't give much serious attention to anything beyond what takes place within the context of human life, based upon what the senses can gather and what the human mind can paint. For the blues, life typically revolves around the mundane and ordinary—finding in them the "stuff" that makes life both enjoyable and lamentable.

It might go too far to label these various blues artists and cultural critics "humanists"—a term foreign to many of them. Nonetheless, it is safe to say these figures—both named and unnamed—in their music champion sensibilities and aims that jibe with what we now reference as humanistic inclinations. Their songs offer morals and life lessons that dismiss a theistic worldview and instead enhance the integrity of life while pushing for the humanity of people of African descent within death-dealing social arrangements. The aim of so many of these musically expressed stories entails a sense of human development and yearning within the context of human history—nothing transhistorical, nothing transcendent. These morality songs mark an early indication that humanist sensibilities couched in a coded philosophy of life are found in African American communities early in (if not before) the history of the United States.

To be clear: before the development of secular government as outlined in the Declaration of Independence and the U.S. Constitution, enslaved Africans mapped out a philosophy of life—using the humanist sensibilities lodged in a blending of African culture and "new world" arrangements. What they offered isn't quite Protagoras's pronouncement—later stated by Corliss Lamont—that the human "is the measure of all things." Rather than strong hints of Enlightenment individualism, the humanist-like sensibilities found in African American cultural production recognize more often the individual within the context of community consistent with the West African philosophical principles that inform this "American" development of humanism. African Americans used the tools they possessed and the resources available to them to craft a way of "touching" the world.

Along with music, narratives and stories using animal figures such as "Bre'r Rabbit" don't use contemporary language associated with humanist organizations. Yet, their emphasis on humans working within the confines of what we can know empirically is a theme in line with basic humanist sensibilities. There are ways in which some of these stories, certainly not all, signify supernatural claims and belittle those who wait on the fulfillment of cosmic promises. These more "earthly" stories give a different moral: they suggest we use our creativity, ingenuity, and our own abilities to make whatever we can of the world, and they measure success not with dreams of heavens but through attention to empirically verifiable developments. In addition to these more poetic and fictional accounts, there are personal narratives whose philosophy runs contrary to theistic traditions present in the United States. Think, for instance, in terms of the various writings of abolitionist Frederick Douglass. Some debate his disbelief because he, at times, indicates he isn't opposed to Christianity that doesn't support slavery, that doesn't allow abuse of black bodies while claiming righteousness, and so on. But think about that statement in a couple of ways.

First, it's political. Douglass understands the manner in which religiosity was often assumed—just as it is today—as a marker of moral standing. There was an assumption on the part of too many that theism provided the moral outlook and conviction necessary to motivate structural change. Churches provide organizational frameworks and a leadership financial independent of government, etc., and this served as an early method of social protest as noted in the first chapter. Many have tended to think about social justice in terms of Christian leadership and theistic organizations. In so doing, there has been a particular theism-biased narrative of justice work and one gets a good sense of this in terms of long gaps between recognized humanism and principled leadership on issues of race. Seeming to not be opposed to religion was a move made in order to assure access to particular communities and conversations.

Second, the Christianity Douglass says he doesn't mind doesn't exist: what is an example of Christianity without these defects? Not even the Bible—the source of inspiration, rules, and regulations for Christians—is devoid of these flaws. So, he expresses willingness to give the nod to a form of Christianity that doesn't exist. And this leaves him free to maintain his more empirical and materialistic worldview, and still come across as not being hostile toward theism. More impressive than his turning of phrase as political act, however, is his language that speaks solidly to a humanistic perspective lodged within the grammar of Christianity. Related to this, Douglass indicates at one point he prayed for many years, but didn't receive an answer until he prayed with his legs. Deciphered: Human activity is the only way to achieve anything. Don't rely on supernatural assistance.

Frederick Douglass yes, but what about others before a long leap to figures like Baynard Rustin? Is this gap a lack of presence or a lack of perspective on how humanism develops outside predominantly white communities? Does this gap stem from oversights based on the assumed look and location of humanism? Or, is the gap substantive in that there really isn't a noteworthy presence to discuss and celebrate? My opinion on this is simple: the gap isn't real; it's a lack of perspective matched by a rather lazy and Eurocentric take on who can really handle all the heady dimensions of humanism.

Part of the mistake has been to assume anyone who discusses African American theistic traditions and does so without venomous mocking must adhere to what she describes. This, for instance, is the method by which W. E. B. Du Bois is so often labeled a "Christian." He wrote about the potential of black churches to help advance the struggle for racial justice based on numbers, economics, and tradition. Yet, Du Bois—whose early acquaintance with church he acknowledges as limited—notes he lost any regard for Christianity as a student studying in Germany. The first African American to secure the PhD from Harvard University, Du Bois knew the Pragmatic tradition. Of course this is the case in that he did some of his intellectual training with pragmatist thinker William James. Within Du Bois' work is a key turn marked by focused attention on what was empirically variable. In fairness, this alone doesn't point to his humanist-type inclinations. What does point in this direction are his own words in volumes such as his autobiographical treatment titled *Dusk of Dawn*.

He regards as important the religion (i.e., theistic systems) of African Americans because of its cultural significance, but not because it houses substantive truth claims. Du Bois is concerned with the progression of human life by means of reason, ingenuity, and creativity, or what he calls "the *souls* of Black Folk." Souls . . . he isn't speaking to a theistically inspired something, some spiritual "thing" residing in the body until death. Rather, he means something more humanistic—the genius or talents of a particular community by means of which it contributes to world civilization. Du Bois held principles that we, at this moment in history, might understand as humanistic in nature and orientation. And what is important about this is the fact that this secularist, this thinker whose philosophy lines up with much of what we would call humanism, defined the nature of race and racism in the twentieth century. He wrote, in 1903, that "the problem of the twentieth century is the color line," and this color line shapes contemporary perceptions of how and why race matters. To talk about race in the twenty-first century is, in important ways, to bring into play the perceptions of life offered by an African American nontheist.

After Du Bois' *Souls of Black Folk* (1903), in which he theorizes the nature and meaning of race, there begins a noteworthy political turn in African American politics. A segment of the African American population embraced dimensions of Marxism and advocated for a modified socialism. Some of the figures moving in this political direction were churchmen, such as Reverdy C. Ransom of the African Methodist Episcopal Church, the oldest African American denomination in the United States. However, others saw this turn to socialist frameworks of political activity as demanding an understanding of theistic organizations as having value only as a space for gathering to coordinate political praxis. Figures who held to this second perspective critiqued the theology and metaphysical assumptions of black churches and left behind theism as a faith stance for the empirical realities of life and the ability of determined humans to shape their own destiny. They challenged black churches and their leadership, exposing their inability to fully engage labor and economic issues because of a theology of suffering focused on a correction of current circumstances not in this world but the "next." This wasn't the perspective of all black churches, but it was prevalent enough to catch the attention of these radical thinkers and activists.

This turn to Marxism, or socialism, and in some cases communism, marked an important undercurrent of twentieth-century African American opposition to theism. And, politically articulated nontheism carries forward into the late twentieth century through public leaders such as A. Philip Randolph, a major player in the labor movement and the civil rights movement. Today, some humanists and atheists claim President Barack Obama, yet he labels himself a Christian. His rhetoric would suggest his thinking is in fact Christian to the extent it is in line with the social gospel, which understands the Christian faith at its best to be about the uplift of the oppressed. Rather than pointing to Obama, I would instead highlight the ongoing importance of humanistic-inclined activists such as Angela Davis as a better representation of politicized nonbelief, and as an important marker of the ongoing legacy of African American political engagement without belief in God. Furthermore, James Foreman, who delivered the "Black Manifesto" speech at Riverside Church (NYC) in which he demands religious organizations pay back African Americans for the years of financial benefit they've secured from their participation in racism, is an important champion of humanism. His work in the civil rights movement through the Student Nonviolent Coordinating Committee was fueled in large part by a politicized worldview stemming from an early rejection of the God idea.

The twentieth century witnessed the emergence of a rich and robust literary movement expressed in concert with significant political developments. This movement, the "Renaissance," covered a significant region of the East—moving from the Washington, DC area to its epicenter in Harlem, New York, and west toward Chicago. One of the well-known figures of this movement is Zora Neale Hurston, whose books such as *Jonah's Gourd Vine* have endured over the years. What is often forgotten is her rather humanistic inclinations. For instance, although as an anthropologist she studied the religious traditions of African Americans in the Deep South (e.g., Florida) and participated in the activities of Voodoo, she is also known to have believed prayer was for the weak minded in that it was a crutch for those who were unwilling to rely on human ingenuity and potentiality.

Like Hurston, writers such as Richard Wright and Langston Hughes explored religion. How or why would they avoid a discussion of religion when the landscape of African American communities as well as the terrain of African American imagination is so broadly marked by theism? Yet, they explored religion—particularly Christianity—in a critical manner, dismantling it and rejecting it. Examples of this rejection include Hughes' famous (or infamous depending on one's perspective) poem "Goodbye Christ," in which he pushes aside attention to Christianity in favor of the potential benefit of Marxism. Hughes, under pressure from the McCarthy purge, would argue the poem and his personal inclinations didn't move in the direction of atheism and communism, but his biting critique of Christianity in this poem and other stories and novels provides a powerful counter position. Wright's novels such as *Black Boy (American Hunger)* reject Christianity's delusional depiction of life in favor of a more existentialist take on life. His writing, in this regard, is akin to that of figures such as Albert Camus. And there's good reason for this. For example, both grew up within a context of poverty, with some health challenges, and family structures that worked against critical thinking. Both found a form of resistance and struggle in writing, and both found writing much more freeing than the Christian faith.

It isn't the case that all these figures had long lives, but they had influential lives—helping to shape popular perceptions of race, gender, and class within the United States. One who died before producing a wealth of literature is Lorraine Hansberry. Still, her play presented on Broadway and still of great interest to American theater, *A Raisin in the Sun*, tells the story of an African American family struggling against the race and class restrictions of life in the form of housing covenants. Much of the action of the book takes place within their living room, and the conversations are laced with biting critiques of theism through which Hansberry—like Frederick Douglass—privileges the work of humans and pushes against giving cosmic "stuff" credit for what humans work to accomplish. The humanism in such a position on struggle and activism is telling. And of course, this trail of humanist literature has to include more recent developments such as the award-winning text by Ta-Nehisi Coates, *Between the World and Me*. It is an inspired discussion of race and its impact on life within the United States. What humanists and atheists have rightly noted, in addition to the insights on race, is the manner in which his perspective draws from humanist sensibilities.

African Americans weren't the only population concerned with issues of justice and influenced by Marxist and socialist thought. Think in terms of the Chicano movement that tracks along a time frame similar to the African American civil rights movement. While some figures working to better the sociopolitical and economic well-being of Latinos/as, such as Cesar Chavez, didn't necessarily discard Christianity (largely Roman Catholicism), this isn't to say all Latino/a activists working on issues of racial and class justice were theists. We've set the record straight in terms of African American activism; the same correction has to be made concerning Latino/a activism: it wasn't all Christian inspired and orchestrated. The nationalist impulse—*La Raza*—meant to rethink the life conditions of Chicanos gave ample attention to socialist philosophy in ways that didn't collapse into theistic notions of history, community, and human progress. It involved a critique of capitalism and strategies of struggle with deep nontheistic roots and motivations. Or, one might consider figures such as Bill Flores, who was involved in the League of Revolutionary Struggle. As a communist, he likely did not believe the advancement of Chicanos required (or even benefitted from) theistic sensibilities. His is a communist approach to transformation that has little room for the traditions of theism as anything more than a problem to solve.

Such thinking fueled not only African American and Chicano struggle for racial justice, but also informed the work of a population whose contact with white supremacy involved not "black" or "brown" pride, but rather the embrace of "red" bodies as valuable beyond the status quo. The American Indian movement (AIM), initiated in the late 1960s, may embrace spirituality, but it defines spirituality as promoting connection between all Indian peoples. It promotes not a separation from the world but rather a shared sense of community within an existential context and as combat against historical circumstances. It's a spirituality that pushes for self-determination as the outcome and scope of work—not some type of otherworldly reward. Spirituality, in this context, seems more cultural than metaphysical in a traditionally theistic way. Hence, it is a critique of Western metaphysics, politics, economics, and culture in favor of something more authentic to American Indians and more restorative of their collective wellbeing. AIM didn't rule out the participation of traditional spiritual leaders in activism, but their involvement speaks to recognition of the ancestors, of the history of the people, and of the nature of communal relationships. It is about embracing the cultural heritage of the people. For instance, notions of the sacred have as much to do with the locations of profound human interactions as with anything else. Sacred spaces are locations not so much where something beyond human reach—gods and goddesses—met humankind. Rather, the sacred has to do with connections between humans and the environment. Constituted by this interaction is a deep and rich regard for human relationship with the various modalities of historically situated life.

Humanistic activism extends beyond African Americans, Hispanics, and American Indians. For example, Dr. Grace Lee Boggs grew up in the Northeast, New York City, and experienced racism against people of Chinese descent. After receiving her PhD in philosophy, she took employment at the University of Chicago library and engaged in social activism, including tenants' rights campaigns. She joined the Workers Party. Her activism put her in touch with central figures such as C. L. R. James. She moved back to New York City, where she continued her work on racial and economic justice. She eventually settled in Detroit, where she continued this activism, including the development of an award-winning youth program. Her thought and activism were deeply influenced by secular and atheist philosophical perspectives.

Of course, it's important to note the humanist inclination of contemporary figures. But we do a disservice if we don't recognize the manner in which current voices echo centuries-old patterns of nontheistic thinking and doing. White humanists may have recently recognized the existence of African American humanists, Hispanic humanists, and so on; but that recent recognition shouldn't be confused with a moment of creation. White recognition didn't create these humanists "of color" (a phrase I detest) any more than the arrival of European explorers marked the creation of the Americas. What it points to is historical shortsightedness.

As a connected point, the limited number of racial minorities in the majority of humanist organizations doesn't speak in a significant way to the viability or historical presence of humanism within the communities and collective memory of these racial minorities. Why don't racial minorities—marking a growing population in more than one way—belong in more substantive numbers to organizations committed to humanist thought and activism? There is an assumption racial minorities are missing out on opportunities, are ignoring important connections, but are they?

I raise these questions and say what I say not to dismiss these organizations. In fact, I work with many of them. Rather, the aim is perspective—to recalculate how and why these organizations seek a more diverse population and to begin that process by getting rid of a perspective that assumes the territory (read the relationship between humanism and the communities of racial minorities) is new and untapped.

The trails of humanism are varied and move through numerous locations. Humanism comes in many shapes and sizes, and is expressed using a variety of cultural codes and grammars. Organizations wanting to reenvision their membership do well to recognize this and attempt to learn these codes and grammars by first paying attention to histories other than their own.

* * *

If You Want to Know More

Without a doubt, the history of humanism within racial minority communities is long and deep. Here are some materials that will fill in gaps and tell you a bit more about this history than the above discussion can due to space limitations.

Boggs, Freddy Paine and Lyman Paine. *Conversations in Maine: Exploring Our Nation's Future* (Boston, MA: South End Press, 1978).

Boggs, Grace Lee. *Living for Change: An Autobiography* (Minneapolis, MN: University of Minnesota Press, 2013).

Boggs, Grace Lee. *The Next American Revolution: Sustainable Activism for the Twenty-First Century* (Berkeley, CA: University of California Press, 2012).

Bolívar, Simón (edited by David Bushnell). *El Libertador: Writings of Simón Bolívar* (New York: Oxford University Press, 2003).

Bullivant, Stephen and Michael Ruse, editors. *The Oxford Handbook of Atheism* (New York: Oxford University Press, 2016), section 6 ("Global Expressions").

Coates, Ta-Nehisi. *Between the World and Me* (New York: Spiegel and Grau, 2015).

Jackson, Richard L. *Black Literature and Humanism in Latin America* (Athens, GA: University of Georgia Press, 2008).

Johansen, Bruce E. *Encyclopedia of the American Indian Movement* (Santa Barbara, CA: Greenwood, 2013).

Lackey, Michael. *African American Atheists and Political Liberation: A Study of the Sociocultural Dynamics of Faith* (Gainesville, FL: University Press of Florida, 2007).

Marti, José. *Selected Writings* (New York: Penguin, 2002).

Munoz, Carlos. *Youth, Identity, Power: The Chicano Movement* (New York: Verso, 2007).

Pinn, Anthony B., guest editor. "The Colors of Humanism," a special issue of *Essays in the Philosophy of Humanism* 20, no. 1 (June 2012).

Pinn, Anthony B. *By These Hands: A Documentary History of African American Humanism* (New York: New York University Press, 2002).

Smith, Paul Chaat and Robert Allen Warrior. *Like a Hurricane: The Indian Movement from Alcatraz to Wounded Knee* (New York: The New Press, 1997).

SECTION TWO
Addressing Racism

4

THE NATURE OF PRIVILEGE

White privilege isn't about having wealth. No, it's about the positive assumptions that follow and inform life for white Americans. It's the often unspoken and unrecognized access to the workings of social life that come with the membership card of whiteness.

Here's the question: what of this privilege are you willing to surrender in order to promote equality and justice, and what is gained by doing the right thing regarding the negative effects of privilege?

* * *

The more graphic markers of racial injustice—such as racialized slavery—no longer define U.S. collective life. However, centuries of racism and its practice entail the development and exercise of privilege that many citizens ignore.

Let's start with a basic statement for context: race-based privilege isn't **lodged only** in wealth and material "stuff" possessed. It isn't simply the ability to buy things or in other ways secure goods. This isn't a matter of financial well-being, how much money one has in the bank. So, one can be economically challenged, white, and still privileged because in the United States it isn't assumed that the economic condition of a white person speaks a fundamental truth about their very being, who she or he is in an inherent way. So many assume that acquisition (or class status) defines privilege due in part to the fact that we have caste progress in terms of economic health. As a consequence, much less attention is given to larger issues of identity that shape how rich or poor people are understood, valued, and appreciated . . . or not.

Think about the above in light of questions asked commonly with energy and with sincerity: "My family didn't have slaves . . . why is racism my problem?" Or, with even more passion and confusion: "We have a black president, what more do you want?" I get why people ask these questions and others like them, but I also understand that such questions (sincere or not) fail to recognize the nature of privilege in the United States. That is to say, whiteness comes with a range of perks not deciphered by gauging who owned plantations and who didn't. Some of them are obvious—e.g., standards of beauty geared toward that population, and more economic success on average are but two. (Keep in mind I didn't write economics don't matter. No, I said privilege isn't simply lodged *only in* economics.) However, there are also "soft," or less easily articulated, forms of privilege that are often ignored: the assumption the police are there to serve and protect; the assumption you weren't placed near the restroom in the restaurant because of skin color; the belief you should be able to drive a luxury vehicle without people assuming you are a drug dealer; the notion you should be successful and it's a problem if you aren't; the assumption you are included in the "we" that defines citizenship in the United States; and, the belief your well-being is fundamental to "making America great again." Privilege allows for these assumptions or principles to be understood as "givens."

This is not to say race alone amounts to the playground for white privilege. No, privilege as discussed in this chapter informs and shapes a variety of additional social constructions—including gender, sexuality, and class. Other volumes in this series will tackle such realities, so here I limit the subject to white privilege as it works through the category of race.

Sure, not all white Americans are wealthy and protected, but even so their whiteness is not used as proof-positive of inherent inferiority. Whiteness isn't used as the reason why they aren't successful. White Americans aren't defined by the worst of their circumstances. No one says, "Well, that poor behavior is what you can expect . . . after all, he's white." Who looks at a white American accused of murder, or robbery, etc., and assumes that is how *all* white Americans behave? Who looks at a white American television character and assumes the character is a true-to-form representation of *all* white Americans? The answer to these questions: no one. However, with respect to racial minorities the answer is different . . . too often very different.

Again, what are your considerations when you buy a car, and do they include how much police attention you'll receive? If you are placed near the restrooms in a restaurant, what's your first thought? If you ask to see an item in a department store and the clerk immediately tells you its expensive before gathering the item, what is your first thought? For racial minorities, these events are likely to trigger particular feelings: frustration, anxiety, annoyance, and anger. Only those whose personhood isn't questioned as a matter of common practice and perception tend to be calm in the face of such events, no matter how small or insignificant the slight might appear.

Privilege is the socially arranged and culturally ingrained assumption that one's perspective is normative, one's importance firm, and one's right to what the United States has to offer beyond question. It's the assumption that when "people of color" are mentioned it means everyone *except* "white" people. And, this thinking isn't questioned in ways that change the dynamics of collective life. Effort to rework this thinking by highlighting the value, importance, and integrity of other communities brings this privilege to the forefront.

Progress on issues of racial justice requires recognizing both the obvious forms of privilege generated by whiteness and also the more covert forms of privilege that mark life in the United States for white Americans. While important as a first step, recognition of privilege isn't sufficient. It isn't the end of struggle, but rather it sets us up to do the required justice work. So, progress toward racial justice means not only recognition of privilege, but also a critique of privilege (in the form of action) by those who benefit from it.

Events such as "Black Lives Matter" and the effort to turn it into "All Lives Matter" have highlighted the ongoing presence and power of white privilege. On the surface, this broader slogan is a way of naming all human lives as valuable, but it hides something. It hides white privilege by not questioning the very reason the "Black Lives Matter" pronouncement matters. It doesn't correct the situation of racial injustice—the manner in which race and racism have defined life in narrow ways for a significant portion of the population. Instead, this seemingly well-meaning shift in emphasis covers up inequalities through a fog of passive language and a quick turning of the tables. This, "Hey, everyone matters!" doesn't allow those who suffer due to the effects of racism to voice their plight. Instead, they are told to get in line behind the "dominant" population. Nothing changes, and white privilege remains the rule of the day—complete with not too subtle a suggestion that the "Black Lives Matter" struggle is actually divisive and a problem that does more damage than the conditions it seeks to address. Those who point out violence against blacks are marked as causing hostility because they are the source of discord. In an odd twist, then, those who seek to maintain things as they are in the form of the racial status quo come off as unifiers who are the true champions of democracy and individual well-being. Those suggesting this sort of "inclusive" rhetoric come to the strategy and the assumptions it safeguards based on a long history of whiteness as the mark of belonging, as the best symbol of civilization and political-cultural superiority.

Think about the early push of Europeans into North America. They claimed a special status despite their rather marginal (religiously and politically articulated) status back home. The idea of this new land constituting a "city on a hill" established by divine right and meant for the chosen—those who rethought themselves during the long voyage from England, where their religious inclinations made them anything but widely privileged and honored citizens. But in this new land they could reinvent themselves along religious, political, and cultural lines and mark out this new status in part through a process of domination and differentiation between themselves, the American Indians they encountered, and the Africans they would eventually bring in large numbers.

White colonists believed themselves superior because they had the Christian faith, knew civil forms of government, and had the

THE NATURE OF PRIVILEGE • 73

markings of a distinct connection to the divine: they were white "like" the historical Jesus and the mysterious God connected to him. In fact, they understood this connection to the divine meant a special future for them and the right to whatever they desired. We've come to call this way of thinking "Manifest Destiny"—the philosophical or theological position that a particular people—not despite but rather because of their whiteness and what that represented for them—were meant for greatness. They were carrying forward God's attention as a special group for whom God labored. Everything good and desirable was for them, and God was fine with them destroying anything and anyone who stood in the way. For many, this was fueled through direct appeal to the biblical text—drawing from the adventures of the "Children of Israel," who suffered, but whom God loved and eventually gave a great land. They assumed their "discovery"—yes, they thought they'd discovered this land because the indigenous population didn't matter—of the "New World" was cosmically arranged and divinely justified. They came; they saw; they tried to take—and along the way life was lost on both sides of that struggle.

A nation that would become a world power was developed. And, despite the fact that this nation was and is premised upon the workings of a secular government, much of the political and cultural rhetoric framing the United States draws from a theological grammar and vocabulary that maintains the vision of "chosen-ness." Again, the story goes, the white population is blessed with specialness as a select population physically and socially marked for greatness. This language undergirds the mundane activities of the day, giving them a depth by tying them to some grand scheme that puts whites on top, and all others below them.

Perhaps even hints of an economic theology developed in Europe surfaced in this North American white privilege. I have in mind two things: religious reformer John Calvin's perception of predestination and double predestination—the idea that some are meant for hell and others for heaven, and all this in accordance with God's pleasure, God's whim. How does one know who is who? Church attendance and other such practices of religious ritual aren't sufficient evidence. Anyone can go to church, sing songs, or pray. Instead, according to

Calvin and his followers, perhaps God shows those whom God loves (those going to heaven) special favor in the form of success. So, there is a connection between "success" and divine favor. Or, jumping to the twentieth century, the sociologist Max Weber provided a way to think about a rather long history of connection between success and spiritual well-being. All this is to say the special status assumed by those of European descent in the United States is built on a long history that is both religious and secular. And so, attention to economic activity in this capitalist system is tied to the religious-theological assumptions that God's people are to be successful in all areas of life—and those not chosen, not special, are at the service of and are inferior to those whom God loves.

All this entails metaphysical justification for claims that support the dominance of white Americans, and it fuels a range of privileges that have been normalized over the years. The United States has come to embody the assumption that white Americans have built this country and any effort on the part of "nonwhites" might just get a firm push back and the rhetoric typically associated with this push back is this: "take back the country." Or, depending on the "look" of the offender, it might be "go back to your country!" Whatever the language used, the function is the same—to remind all that white is the standard, and whites are with certain rights not afforded necessarily to others unless they become honorary whites. This privilege entails awareness, for instance, of white heroes because they are ever present. It is having one's racial heritage celebrated not one month out of a year, but every day through the general workings of the nation. To wake up and leave the house is, in keeping with white privilege, to be confronted by spaces designed and meant for use and enjoyment by whites.

It's tricky, and I don't write this as a dismissive or paternalistic statement. Rather, there is challenge here in that privilege isn't visible. No, it's the consequences or the attitudinal and material connotations of privilege that frame and impact collective life in the United States. Few whites, I would argue, walk around thinking about their privileges. No, they don't think they're privileged; they simply live these privileges and give all this no more thought then we think about the supply of oxygen we consume from moment to moment, no more than we think about the gravity that keeps us grounded. We aren't aware of them until their existence—or access to them—is threatened. The same is the case with white privilege: it goes without saying, until those who don't benefit from it name it, challenge it, and seek to interrogate it.

White privilege isn't something that whites demand; or something they call for. It just is a basic framing of life within the United States. That's the staying power of privilege. It is that unspoken assumption, the normative claims about certain groups that undergirds their sense of entitlement. It is the ability to walk into a room and assume one "owns it," or at least is "welcomed in it." Or to ask why all the black kids are sitting together, and why they've isolated themselves without seeing white "space" as segregated space. It is the most fundamental distinction between "insiders" and "outsiders" the United States offers. Privilege is fused into even the smallest and most trivial dimensions of personal life and layered across the largest and most significant aspects of collective life. It becomes a way of monitoring which bodies are free to move without restrictions and which bodies must remain in their place.

What I offer here is another way of speaking about the nature of freedom in the United States. Here's one way to get at it: ask racial minorities what they think about national politics, and the answers given likely will in some way incorporate the realities of whiteness. However, ask whites the same questions and the need to take into consideration the impact of racial minorities on their options as whites is less compelling, less central, less often noted.

Privilege—these unstated opportunities and positive assumptions—if not tackled taint justice work by turning attention to whites rather than keeping the focus on the racial minorities most deeply impacted by white privilege. Let's go back to the example I offered earlier: "everyone suffers" or "all lives matter" shifts focus and reinforces the normative standing of whites by moving away from an explicit concern with the injustice of race to the human condition. This move clouds the issue and prevents any real work to dismantle the problems that beset certain communities. Such a move wipes out any starting point for justice work because it marks the entire population as harmed. White privilege is denied in the guise of the human condition, and as consequences those who suffer most from racism are denied opportunity to expose and critique the systemic structures and social assumptions that support their oppression. Once the "all lives matter" rhetoric is deployed—like a bucket of cold water—any effort to subvert that generalization so as to support racial minorities who encounter racism in particular ways comes across as aggressive, counterproductive, racist and destructive . . . and nothing changes. Here's the proverbial elephant in the room: **"white" Americans *are* raced.** White privilege is meant to hide this fact, to make it seem as all others are raced but whites just are . . . well, colorless humans.

The markers of white privilege have been a topic of conversation in certain quarters for a good number of years now, and I'm going to draw on those sources in what follows. Perhaps one of the most widely recognized names in the early presentation of this "way" of life is Peggy McIntosh, whose essay "White Privilege and Male Privilege: A Personal Account of Coming to See Correspondences Through Work in Women's Studies" (1988) stirred things up. An excerpt of that longer piece—titled "White Privilege: Unpacking the Invisible Knapsack"—condenses many of the concerns that frame this chapter. In the shorter piece, McIntosh provides a list of twenty-six examples of white privilege, which mark out the socioeconomic, political, cultural, and psychological benefits of whiteness in the United States as the dominant cultural symbol and as a physical majority.

McIntosh begins by pointing out what racial minorities experience: whites are often unaware consciously of privilege but their denial, if not actions, speaks to their reality and a deep desire to protect those advantages birthed through the social construct of cultural whiteness tied to certain physical markers of majority status. McIntosh puts it best when saying, "I have come to see white privilege as an invisible package of unearned assets which I can count on cashing in each day, but about which I was 'meant' to remain oblivious." And, she continues with a visual, "white privilege is like an invisible weightless knapsack of special provisions, maps, passports, codebooks, visas, clothes, tools and blank checks." All these provide access to and transport around the various geographies of life in the United States.

Often these privileges are unacknowledged because they are coded into the very rights of citizenship in this country, and there is an assumption that postslavery (and other racial atrocities) these rights are available to all. Yet, while in theory this is the case, in practice full access to the "goods" and "grammars" of American life remain restricted and accessed by a particular membership card given to some at birth and denied others. Sure, some African Americans, some Latino/s, some American Indians, some Asian Americans, and so on, have the markers of success. And this is because economic success isn't the only marker of this privilege. So, Asian Americans can have a median household income higher than the white population (according to some sources), and still face disadvantage because privilege has social-cultural dimensions not tied to a paycheck. Economic success doesn't prevent having one's identity determined by (or at least measured against) stereotypical depictions of one's racial group, for instance. The general practices of life in the United States still disadvantage racial minorities.

What is more, the failure of racial minorities to achieve is assumed a marker of a general and intrinsic inferiority, while this perspective isn't generally applied in the case of white Americans who don't succeed. Whites remain understood as entitled and the failure to access what they are entitled to isn't a permanent stain on them. These, as McIntosh notes, are unearned advantages, the "stuff" that comes along with being born into the white race, and these unearned privileges can wreak harm on other racial groups that don't share these advantages.

The idea, then, is to recognize these unearned privileges and work to neutralize them, to develop approaches to life that allow for the advancement of all groups based, as Dr. Martin L. King, Jr., would note, on the "content of character." So, the challenge is to *recognize* white privilege and *react* in ways that maintain this uncomfortable awareness, and *rework* systemic structures of collective life in such a way as to decrease white privilege and maximize the well-being of all.

It is too often the case, from my vantage point, that humanists assume denial of privilege is enough to end practices of privilege. Untrue, as McIntosh argues, such a stance serves to reenforce privilege by denying where it is present and how it works. Acknowledging privilege is insufficient in and of itself. As Fredrick deBoer remarks in a *Washington Post* piece ("Admitting That White Privilege Helps You Is Really Just Congratulating Yourself") that references the work of philosopher George Yancy, acknowledging privileges, lamenting them even, without reaction and reworking systemic realities simply keeps focus on whites and makes all circumstances about them. Yes, point out the problem, but don't assume this is the end of one's obligations as opposed to simply an invitation to get to work. One cannot dismantle structures without first acknowledging their existence and felt consequences.

Humanists, as reasonable people, make this first step—based only on my limited experience—without a great deal of difficulty; and it's expressed implicitly through a variety of conference presentations by people they pay to be told of their privilege. And, there is also the explicit recognition of white privilege in personal and collective ways as well. Yet, the next step can be a bit of a challenge in part because of organizational agendas: the more easily targeted separation of church and state issue, science education, and so on. These don't pull personally, don't require so much in the same way so they are the fall-back position. But, there's more required—much more, actually.

While deBoer argues against any use of public "self-indictment," I wouldn't go so far. Rather, as Yancy, I would encourage humanists to understand it as a necessary first step, the first effort to pull back the curtain, so to speak, and remove the stumbling block of denial. The key is to not stop with that acknowledgment as if the purpose of such an acknowledgment is to somehow make things better by the privileged person realizing the existence of privilege. I understand that some might find this stance problematic in that it, they might argue, comes too close to a sense of "original sin" about which whites can do little. This, however, isn't what I have in mind. Privilege isn't a theologically contrived notion that highlights a mark on one's "soul." No, privilege is a system of social arrangements into which one is born. We are born into circumstances that shape our approach to life and the parameters of that life—just as we are born into particular families, in particular cities, in a particular country. The task for those who recognize the downside of this social system is to do something about it. To simply state the existence of privilege is to attempt to distance one's white-self from other whites by making oneself part of "us" rather than "them" (i.e., the privileged). This alone will only hide privilege in plain sight, once again. Rather, expose the privilege; expose what is unearned and in this way create a space for doing something as a next step.

In certain ways, McIntosh, Yancy, deBoer, and I are interested in the same thing: exposing white privilege as real, developing strategies to decrease its negative impact, and working to shift the focus for this activity to the racial minorities harmed by white privilege, to make them the center of conversation. One should think about this not strictly in terms of the loss of privilege but rather as a gain, as advancement in that diversity of perspective and opinion is actually strength. By not thinking too highly of oneself, there is a counterinvitation for racial minorities to move away from thinking too little of themselves in line with racial oppression and the status quo. As a result, by acknowledging privilege and supporting equity, we work toward the full humanity of all as accountable and responsible agents in the world. Within the context of humanist organizations and communities, there are numerous ways to tackle this work on white privilege. Here are just a few:

1. *Make acknowledgment of white privilege central to the missions and aims of humanist organizations and communities.* That is to say, through such a naming of white privilege within the context of collective self-understanding, it becomes possible to understand the dismantling of white privilege and fundamental to self-understanding and operational success. To fail on this front is to fail on a collective level. This renders addressing white supremacy not an organizational "footnote" but rather a central element of our collective prose. Recognition of white privilege deconstructs something of what it means to be white and by extension forces a reconfiguration of white identity. Racial minorities are required

constantly to wrestle with who they are, what they are worth, and where they belong. Acknowledging, no, denouncing, white privilege will force those taking this stand to also rethink their sense of being on a deep level. To the extent white privilege has defined white life, challenging it also challenges identity, purpose, and place for whites.

2. *Contextualize this acknowledgment of white supremacy.* In other words, this public recognition of a problem must be tied to particularities of life, and can't be a general statement that doesn't target real situations and concerns. Those sorts of abstract statements simply cloud the issues, preventing substantial thinking and working because they give no base upon which to ground praxis. Speak in detail and in light of particulars. This also involves recognizing that white privilege can be addressed, can be tackled, but doing so requires recognition that these privileges attach to physical and cultural constructed bodies. And, these bodies move through the world within particular geographies and locales and in connection to real, historical realities.

3. *Invite the participation of racial minorities in this process not to make those with white privilege feel better, or to comfort them, but rather to point ways forward by centralizing the concerns and insights of those who suffer from white privilege.* It is often the case that racial minorities are invited to participate in humanist organizations and communities through speeches, panels, and so on. These activities are often meant to point out racism and to speak to how humanists might think about their role. But too often, at least in my experience, these sessions easily devolve into opportunities for white participants to take roll call on all the ways in which they have fought racism. While they may in fact have worked to dismantle racism, it doesn't mean they have acknowledged sufficiently their participation in white supremacy: so they address the symptoms without addressing the cause. And in the end, they believe they have accomplished something.

4. *React and act mindful of particularities by targeting particular manifestations of white privilege, and in so doing follow the lead of racial minorities.* This is a hard step to be sure. However, steps 1–3 hold little meaningful promise if they aren't matched by an effort to actively address particular manifestations of white supremacy. So, for instance, if within your particular area one of the significant manifestations of privilege involves issues of housing, address it by targeting both formal and informal regulations that prevent racial minorities from being in and feeling comfortable within particular neighborhoods.

5. *Determine the most prudent outlets for this dismantling of privilege work.* There's a need to be strategic about this work and there is a need for it to be organic. By that I mean to say focus on areas of privilege that have significant impact within your region or area, and make use of approaches that are tailored to those problems as they manifest in that particular area/region. In a word, it may not be enough to simply borrow blueprints from others. All of this will involve those with privilege taking their instructions from racial minorities who suffer from the ill effects of white privilege. To assume they, whites with privilege, get to set the terms and determine the strategies simply reenforces the type of dominance and normativity this work is meant to deconstruct. Part of this process has to involve surrender of the assumption that whites (for whatever reason) are best equipped to speak and lead. The normative look of leadership as white has to be broken by literally diversifying the boards of our organizations, the chairs of various committees, and so on. Only when racial minorities hold more involved positions of authority will this attention to white privilege not amount to celebration of the privileged.

6. *Repeat steps 1–5 again ... and again.* White privilege has developed and been refined over the course of centuries, becoming so intrinsic to the "American way of life" that it need not be consciously appealed to for implementation. In fact, to consciously appeal to it results in a critique, even from others who benefit from it. One need only think about the reaction to various

white supremacist groups for evidence of this. No, white privilege operates through silence and assumption, and doesn't need to call attention to itself in order for it to hold sway. These privileges run deep and, as I've already noted, are exercised without thought. This being the case, it won't be easy to limit their impact. It will take ongoing effort and consistent activity with success determined by meaningful progress rather than quick outcomes. There will be setbacks and missteps, but the work needs to be consistent and marked by persistence, and a setting of goals that highlights discernable advancement (e.g., diversity in the leadership of our organizations; more than racial minorities lecturing on racial justice; strong public statements from our organizations in response to racial injustice; significant organizational resources devoted to racial justice work; and strong partnerships with racial justice organizations) over the long haul.

This is not to assume, however, that all racial minorities see white privilege in the same way. Some buy into the white privilege framework for a variety of reasons and actually work to maintain it without substantial damage to it—only want inclusion, or honorary whiteness. In certain quarters this perspective on the part of racial minorities is termed internalized racism, which entails a socialization process by means of which white privilege is assumed correct by the racial minorities who identify with the privileged.

Still, these steps involve something of a new approach to the world, a different way of engaging the world with greater sensitivity to what my grandmother noted as "moving through the world knowing your footsteps matter." It's a pulling back of the cultural curtain and exposing the machinery that has determined the arrangements of life based on color.

Talk of diversity, appreciation of difference, is at best difficult but more likely impossible as values and practices without firm and consistent attention to white privilege—what it offers whites and what it denies racial minorities in the United States. As I've suggested throughout this chapter, racial disparity is a symptom of a larger problem, and that problem is white privilege, which easily supports—

although not always—white supremacy. I make this qualification because I am in no way arguing that the challenge of race and the embrace of privilege within the American Humanist Association is the same as that within the KKK, for instance. Not at all! Instead, I am simply arguing for recognition of a problem and an approach that is dualistic: an attack on what racial minorities don't have access to, and that to which whites have access. Such deconstruction makes space for reconstruction. In this way, it becomes easier to see an attack on white privilege not simply as whites losing something, but rather as the nation gaining something—gaining fuller input from and inclusion of a diversity population. As part of this process, and within the conversations that are sure to ensue, I would suggest removing certain terms and phrases from the accepted language for conversation:

1. *People of color*—this term tends to assume racial minorities are the only raced groups, as if whites aren't also connected to the social construction of race.

2. *We are all oppressed*—this phrase, lodged in slogans such as "all lives matter," is factual on a certain level, but it does little to acknowledge the advantages afforded through whiteness.

3. *I'm color-blind*—on the surface this might sound like progress, but in reality it keeps whiteness normative. It treats, as I've cautioned against throughout this book, difference as a problem to solve as opposed to an opportunity for expansion and growth. When rendered a problem, the logical course of action is to solve it, and in the United States—based on the workings of race and white privilege—this fix maintains the centrality of whiteness in that the fix is to make racial minorities more like whites. And, only in rare cases (the entertainment world holds some), to embrace and absorb the "exotic" by claiming the racial codes and language of the intriguing "other" group. Even this—whites "talking black" or embracing the aesthetics of various racial minority groups—destroys difference by placing cultural resource of racial minorities within the orbit of whiteness. White privilege, then, continues to rule the day.

4. *I'm uncomfortable*—this is really a nonstatement, an emotional marking that has little significance. I say this not to be cruel or to deny the emotional and physiological toll recognizing and challenging privilege entails. All this is real, and I acknowledge that is the case. My rejection of this phrase stems from what it assumes: it assumes that this type of transformation can take place in a way that leaves people comfortably situated, with intact all that is familiar. No, this type of work entails discomfort. In fact, there is good reason to believe you are doing the hard work of exposing and addressing white privilege when there is discomfort. To do good work on the issue, it can't be avoided. Discomfort is a natural component of this work, and I share this thinking with a variety of others writing on this topic of white privilege. Whites will be uncomfortable because the advantages that have worked for them that have nothing to do with merit or "know how" are exposed and called into question. And, racial minorities will be uncomfortable and perhaps angry because the pain they've experienced is brought up fresh and their suspicions concerning the nature of their disadvantage is confirmed, and, for others, because the measures of success and inclusion they've embraced are now called into question.

5. *We've had a black president*—this is indeed a wonderful fact. It marks something of a political-cultural change, but it doesn't indicate the destruction of white privilege and racism. Both survived President Barack Obama's presidency. The function of whiteness in the United States allows exceptions. It constructs situations in which space is made for the "exceptional" situation or person who is believed (at least subconsciously) to reenforce the markers of whiteness—e.g., proper education, proper aesthetic, and so on. Such arrangements don't damage fundamentally the workings of white privilege, but they can trouble those who hold those privileges. One need only think in terms of the resistance to President Obama over the course of his eight years—e.g., Tea Party activities and the unprecedented congressional effort to dismantle any advances he made despite how they might benefit

constituencies. It is so very reasonable to argue some of this resistance extends beyond the scope of politics to the realm of privilege and who should have access to it. All this is to say it will take more than a black president to destroy white privilege and its symptom called racism.

I have argued and continue to believe it is this type of work that highlights the human in *human*ism—the manner in which rejection of supernaturalism and cosmic orchestration of the world puts humans squarely in the center of any and all efforts to improve quality of life and the well-being of all. I imagine some won't agree with this assessment, and within humanist circles this might be a topic for discussion and debate. And part of that discussion might involve why the charge of white privilege elicits a negative response. Such conversation is important and should happen within humanist circles. However, when humanists speak longingly for growth within their ranks and more diverse ranks, attention to issues of white privilege becomes a necessary tactic and more than this, tackling white supremacy has to become a central marker of humanism's identity and purpose.

* * *

If You Want to Know More

I've offered in this chapter information meant to create a particular type of dissonance—the type that exposes examples of how social codes and practices shape life options for white Americans and racial minorities. It might be new information for some, and it might frame the issues differently than had been initially thought by still others. Either way, what I've written will need expansion and clarification. For those interested in more information, I'd suggest the following materials as a good starting point.

Baldwin, James. *The Fire Next Time* (New York: Vintage, 1992).

Driscoll, Christopher. *White Lies: Race and Uncertainty in the Twilight of American Religion* (New York: Routledge, 2015).

Gulati-Partee, Gita and Maggie Potapchuk, "Paying Attention to White Culture and Privilege: A Missing Link to Advancing Racial Equity," *The Foundation Review* 6, no. 1 (2014): 25–38.

Jensen, Robert. *The Heart of Whiteness: Confronting Race, Racism, and White Privilege* (San Francisco: City Lights Publishers, 2005).

Katznelson, Ira. *When Affirmative Action Was White: An Untold History of Inequality in Twentieth-Century America* (New York: W. W. Norton & Company, 2006).

McIntosh, Peggy. "White Privilege and Male Privilege: A Personal Account of Coming to See Correspondences Through Work in Women's Studies," Wellesley College Center for Research on Women (1988).

McIntosh Peggy. "White Privilege: Unpacking the Invisible Knapsack," Wellesley College Center for Research on Women (1988).

Painter, Nell. *The History of White People* (New York: W. W. Norton & Company, 2011).

Roediger, David R. *How Race Survived US History: From Settlement and Slavery to the Obama Phenomenon* (New York: Verso, 2010).

Roediger, David R. *Working Toward Whiteness: How America's Immigrants Became White: The Strange Journey from Ellis Island to the Suburbs* (New York: Basic Books, 2006).

Rothenberg, Paula S. *White Privilege: Essential Readings on the Other Side of Racism* (New York: Worth Publishers, 2015)

Rothman, Joshua. "The Origins of 'Privilege,'" *New Yorker*, May 12, 2014.

Tatum, Beverly Daniel. *Why Are All the Black Kids Sitting Together in the Cafeteria: And Other Conversations About Race* (New York: Basic Books, 2003).

Yancy, George. "Dear White America," *New York Times*, December 24, 2015, http://opinionator.blogs.nytimes.com/2015/12/24/dear-white-america/?_r=0.

5

ON RACIAL KNOWLEDGE

Knowledge is a certain form of power. Humanists read and study. They work based on logic. And, with much energy, they suggest theists do likewise. Logic and reason rule the day.

Here's the question: how much of this call for knowledge, for information, is applied to the issue of race/racism?

* * *

It's the privileges generated by whiteness that matter here—not who owned slaves; it's about what racial discrimination (connected not only to slavery but also to "Jim Crow" regulations and formal policy) has preserved for whiteness. Knowing how this works, how privilege operates, and what racism entails requires some work.

I get it. In fact, it's a natural response—to ask those most familiar with an issue to educate, to guide, *and* to absolve from guilt. African Americans and other racial minorities are familiar with, and to some extent used to, this request. But this entreaty is a bad move, a mistake that can entail laziness. Of course it's lazy when it comes from those who demand others read, study, and analyze. Not all agree with this assessment and instead they might say it's a matter of not knowing where to start, or being overwhelmed by the significant amount of literature available. True, there are numerous books, articles, blog posts, and so on related to race and racism. Academic programs provide courses and academics, journalists, and other commentators offer analysis and reflection broadcast over many radio and television stations on a twenty-four-hour cycle.

Humanists—as far as I can tell—pride themselves on being informed, "well read" on important issues, and always seeking information. In fact, on numerous occasions I've been reminded that nontheists better understand the Bible than theists, and I assume this means they've read it. They read books on scientific developments, and on other secular and significant developments. So, when it comes to race, "I don't know much about African Americans . . ." isn't an acceptable qualifier. That's a stating of the problem—racial ignorance—not a stating of the solution. That type of response, and I mean nothing condescending about this and nothing paternalistic, betrays promise, a reason for hope in what appears a worsening racial environment. Such is the case unless it is quickly followed by "but I know I need to better understand and I'll get on that."

Pulling back the curtain and exposing the problem, seeing how race works in the United States, and understanding that the situation has some bearing on what it means to be a humanist who is committed to humanist values and principles, is important. That effort to self-correct, to gain better context, to critically engage the world beyond one's nose, is important—but where to begin? Where to start? Often the question of where to start simply masks a more problematic take: why start? Why should I have to do any work to understand a problem I didn't create? This is similar to the "I don't own slaves so why should I feel bad about slavery?" response to issues like reparations and any other ongoing discussion of racial justice based on past discrimination.

There are significant holdings related to other areas of concern through which humanists weed without a blank stare and without assuming a "deer in headlights" posture. I'd like to know, but where do I start? Well, I'll tell you where not to start: don't start with the assumption that any racial minority you approach has an obligation to tutor you, to educate you, or worse to absolve you as if to be ignorant is to be guilt-free. Assuming any of these—that anyone you ask owes you what you want, or that not knowing frees you from needing to find out—simply supports and reenforces the type of privilege discussed earlier in the book. And, what is more, such an approach can enhance racism by placing racial minorities back "in the service" of whites. That is to say, whether it's information or some other type of resource—e.g., agricultural stuff, natural resources, and manufactured goods—whites receive it and others provided the labor to make it happen. I don't say this with any animosity. Rather, it is simply a graphic way to name white privilege and what it means, in this case, regarding knowledge of race and racism.

There is something true about the notion that "knowledge is power"—true to the extent that knowledge shapes perception of the world and our relations within it and, by extension, it informs how we move through the world, what we value, what we despise, and what we do with all this. Put differently, knowledge is power because knowledge shapes and programs life—determining what we consider viable options and how we go about securing and working those options.

Surveys and studies speak to levels of racial sensitivity in the United States. For instance, a June 2016 Pew Research Center study titled "On Views of Race and Inequality, Blacks and Whites Are Worlds Apart" indicates that half of those surveyed believe racism in the United States is a problem that requires more attention. And, six out of ten of those surveyed noted attention to racism is required for African Americans to make progress. Race is on the collective mind of the United States, even if the differences between black and white perceptions of racial equality and justice are often vast. Further, debates over the presence of the confederate flag in public spaces and violence against racial minorities such as the deaths of Michael Brown, Eric Garner, and others point to a polarization regarding how to address issues of racial justice vis-à-vis existing systems of law and order. In fact, a December 2014 study conducted jointly by Pew and *USA Today* notes that for many the decision, for instance, not to bring charges against office Darren Wilson in the Michael Brown case was right and that race had little to do with the situation. With respect to Garner, most surveyed didn't see race as a significant factor. Public conversation suggests investigation into the death of Sandra Bland did not yield significantly different perspectives and opinions. Even these few examples suggest an issue for citizens of the United States: racism must be addressed, but evidence of racial violence can be difficult for the population to wrap its mind around. While perceptions of race and racism have altered over time, according to some researchers, we have reached a period of significantly negative perception concerning where this country is in relationship to race and racism. For example, an Associated Press poll from October 2012 notes that, and I'll quote directly here, "in all, 51 percent of Americans now express explicit anti-black attitudes, compared with 48 percent in a similar 2008 survey. When measured by an implicit racial attitudes test, the number of Americans with anti-black sentiments jumped to 56 percent, up from 49 percent during the last presidential election . . ." Ouch. I want to emphasize that the nature of this bias—whether active or passive—is of little importance here. Rather, what remains vital for consideration is simply the fact that such bias exists and is often tied to a lack of information, a dependence on limited knowledge. Tied to this information shortcoming is dependence on longstanding sociocultural codes concerning "blackness" and "whiteness." Racial dynamics in the United States are such that passive embrace of the racial codes seems patriotic, "normal," and highly desirable. Ignorance makes easy this acquiescence to these codes.

U.S. society—for reasons already stated elsewhere in this book—doesn't require every citizen to know and understand race and racism. Substantive discussion of race is missing from most public school curricula, and it tends to occur only in elective courses of study within university and college settings. In fact, one can graduate from college without ever having to devote a noteworthy component of one's course work to the study of race and racial dynamics. Furthermore, while political correctness may prevent some modes of ignorance and abuse, at its worst it stifles attention to open discussion of the hard questions in ways. And, with the latter, it does this by assuming discomfort in such discussions would constitute a problem rather than an important opening for growth. This thinking suggests, at least implicitly, change can be easy—and can be accomplished without much disruption to the way things are currently constituted.

Be nice, and don't really talk about race and racism because it isn't polite (read: comfortable) conversation. Or, when an academic posture is feigned, "we're talking about individual encounters and that's subjective and subjective conversation will get us nowhere." It's not uncommon to hear whispers of "special pleading" when racial minorities speak of hostility and ignorance regarding them. Or, one racial minority may be asked to speak on behalf of an entire race. Any one Latino speaks for all Latinos; or, encountering one Asian Americans tells you about all Asian Americans. This thinking assumes these racial minority communities are monolithic, culturally flat and fixed in history. Such thinking makes it easy to pick out particular moments, isolate them, and ask the random representative about their meaning. The rule is simple: racial minorities suffer from the ill effects of racial discrimination.

There is a manner in which they, racial minorities, reenforce the logic of this race problem through internalized racism, or other ways of accepting the normativity of whiteness. That is to say, racial minorities are encouraged and rewarded for accepting the normativity of whiteness and working to fit that model. These are the "good," "descent," and welcomed minorities that prove the rule concerning the "rest of them." Such "good" racial minorities become a testament to the correctness of white privilege and white supremacy. If members of these groups can be successful by being "like us," then what it means to be "us" has to be significant and superior. This gives the impression that racial discrimination results from the "victims" of it not wanting better, because if they wanted better they could have better. "Just look at Mr. X, who is black and has been successful, or Ms. Y who seems to be doing quite well." Still, when it is all said and done, even these racial minorities who play by the rules suffer from the consequences of a problem not of their construction. They are "successful" within the context of a social world marked by problems of racialization—and their success is always available for inspection, critique, challenge, and removal. "Did I earn this?" "Am I good enough?" are commonly asked questions for this chosen few.

I want to go back to a context briefly noted above, that of higher learning, and I do so for several reasons: (1) it's the context I know best—and, of great importance; (2) it exemplifies both the desire for knowledge and the perpetuation of ignorance that I address within this chapter; and finally, (3) as readers will see later in the chapter, strategies of learning worked out in institutions of higher learning afford valuable lessons for humanists wanting to educate themselves on race. That said, typically the number of racial minorities on the faculty or in senior administrative positions within universities and colleges is so small that racial minority students (a small percentage themselves) can't rely on them to fight their battles against ignorance. Those faculty members and administrators have battles of ignorance to fight. So, colleges and universities by and large are microcosms of the larger society. Serious study of racial minorities is often limited to specialized—and not necessarily well funded—departments and programs that have limited campus reach, or worse, are restricted to offices that really only manage how racial minorities can be aided in "fitting" into campus culture. Or, these offices are established with the idea of addressing their academic weakness and positioning them to take full advantage of the academic opportunity afforded them through affirmative action. Readers should note that here, as too often the case, it is assumed they are there because of affirmative action or quotas—and those who hold this mindset do so without being as aware of "legacy" programs and others modes of affirmative action afforded white Americans. The more things change—increased presence of racial minority students, more engagement between institutions of higher learning and surrounding communities, efforts to recruit faculty to increase faculty diversity—the more they stay the same.

As with the larger society, institutions of higher learning actually change slowly. Campus culture shifts not in real time because the "brand" of the institution is in part its stock and trade. And the "brand" is protected. I'm not suggesting it shouldn't be protected but rather I'm simply suggesting the manner in which the institution's perspective on race is also tied to this brand. That is to say, and the passive voice is important here, academic inquiry is never devoid of racial considerations and accompanying codes learned by simply living in the United States and participating in its life. This isn't hard work; it's just about being present in the United States.

Little victories all framed by the proper rhetoric are celebrated. Nonetheless, the "elephant" in the room remains unnamed, and university or college life works to reenforce problematic assumptions regarding race and racism and in this way prepares generations of new citizens with old problems. In short, ignorance concerning race and racism is acceptable, particularly for those not so deeply impacted by the negative fallout of racial bias. I'm within this environment and have been for a good number of years, and my work revolves around issues of race and the meaning of race, and so I wouldn't say the situation is hopeless, nor would I suggest no meaningful work is being done on college and university campuses. A statement otherwise could be dismissed easily, and should be dismissed.

For sure, there are worthwhile victories being won, but race/racism remains a problem because the structures of life—e.g., social codes, language, cultural norms, and so on—still draw from and reenforce bias. This is the genius behind the race machine in the United States. It self corrects and self perpetuates, and mostly without us giving it a second thought. It all just seems so very natural; the way things are, should be, and will remain. Racial dynamics have taken on a "must be" or fundamental significance in US collective life. These systemic arrangements based on race are understood as necessary, and the idea of change can produce intense discomfort—a visceral response to a challenge to unspoken rules and regulations.

There is a type of "gut knowledge" here, not a sense of social codes expressed through formal instruction but rather through the general process of socialization that takes place through informal conversation, media, and so on. We learn these codes and how to use them without formal preparation or study. They are simply embedded and reenforced in our maturation as social beings in the United States.

This situation of bias is particularly true for the larger population of whites, who can in large part select their interactions with racial minorities. Not understanding race and then being confronted by the consequences of race produces a type of discomfort that gets addressed through silence. Don't talk about it and it will go away; or, only talk about it if absolutely necessary and even then deflect the situation by pointing out the problem as it presents itself elsewhere—

far from home. But still, racial messages are broadcast, received, and processed, if not through formal and critical conversation and study, through popular culture—television, movies, music, and so on. This constitutes an informed ignorance, or an acceptance of absence. It is informed because it is based on external courses, but constitutes ignorance because it does little to expand knowledge of race and racism beyond anecdotal materials, stereotypes confirmed, etc. Now almost all of this falls short of hate crime status that would gain media attention—although hate crimes over the decades have remained fairly steady in the United States. Hate crimes are such because they run contrary to stated regulations and regard for other citizens in ways that have been outlined in law. This informed ignorance is an accepted disregard—the typical state of affairs in race relations USA.

I don't mean to suggest this racial bias amounts to hate crime—to do so, in almost all cases, would be to belittle the tragic and impactful nature of hate crimes. Still, this bias can have felt consequences even if this involves no more than silencing on a localized level racial minorities or reenforcing white privilege and its assumptions concerning links between "color" and social standing (with all that entails). The psychological, emotional, financial, social, and sometimes physical hurt is real, and it lurks even where we think it has been wiped out, or at least dealt with in a meaningful way. One wonders if there is anything that can be done, whether there is a "safe" space free from the turmoil of racial difference made into a problem with dire consequences. One can dream, but, of course, there isn't such a space. Christians might call such a space "heaven," but nontheistic humanists know better. There's no such thing, just spaces where we agree to abide by certain rules of engagement and respect, where we commit to the discomfort that marks work toward the transformation of race and its meaning in the United States.

It isn't clear to me that such an agreement has been reached; there isn't an extensive "space" in which this type of hard work is the standard. The situation is bad. Race relations are in decline from the perspective of a majority of U.S. citizens, as noted in poll after poll, and there is something to this. And, what can be done about this? What's the way forward? Somewhere in the answer to this question should be "study up," learn something about the problems and its various actors. Ask for materials to read, documentaries to watch . . . anything that suggests you are taking responsibility for knowing something about the history and context of racialized life in the United States. Learn something. Read, study, and only then asked informed questions. Show the same commitment to knowing something about race that is shown concerning separation of church and state, evolution, and the other issues that mark the bulk of humanist publications and conference programs. And, these materials aren't simply produced outside the humanist "movement." No, humanist organizations have been bitten by the information-production bug and aren't relying on external mechanisms to produce and distribute information. Think in terms of Prometheus, Humanist Press, and Pitchstone, publisher of this book and the others in this series.

These are just a few examples, just a few of the ways in which humanists (and atheists) produce information. Much of this work involves attention to the sciences, science education, politics, and so on—all topics, again, humanists believe are important to know about, and to know about them is to read about them. This is because it is often the case that the production of knowledge is framed almost exclusively in terms of certain disciplines, and seldom does this constellation of disciplines include the work of figures within the humanities. Sure, humanists give talks, participate in panels, and otherwise are involved in the convention-style exchanges that define much humanist interaction. Still, the dominant intellectual framework highlighted privileges the grammar, vocabulary, and postures of particular laboratory-based sciences. The bias is real, but unnecessary; there is nothing about this bias that is a required dimension of public and private interactions. The humanities, for instance, tell us a great deal about the cultural worlds in which we live, and this information and the ability to engage it critically is vital. Even those within the so-called objective sciences live within cultural worlds that impinge upon investigation. For instance, how else would you explain the Tuskegee Syphilis Experiment or the nineteenth-century scientific developments meant to prove the objective value of what we now call the pseudo-sciences?

It is a given that humanists should expand the topics covered when they read to include issues of race, racism, and whiteness. And, they should not depend on racial minorities to do the heavy lifting for them—to provide living "CliffsNotes" on race. It's more than a little unfair to assume racial minorities should bear the burden of educating whites on issues of race when there's so much information just a bookstore, library, or "click" away. Show some initiative, and demonstrate some commitment and accountability by avoiding the easy path of "hey, racial minority, tell me your story." Do the work; research to find the books, articles, documentaries, and other series discussions of race and whiteness; and tackle these materials. Some of the information discovered will be duds, sure—with little worthwhile content. Not all published materials are equal, and the Internet is a wonderful thing, but there are few checks and balances with regard to quality of materials available. But isn't this uncertainty of information the case with any topic one researches? It isn't unusual, and the charged nature of race and race relations only serve to amplify this situation. This complexity with respect to resources and the inevitability of encountering some duds aren't reason to stop doing the research, but rather are just one of those things that comes with the process of discovery. I don't say this assuming humanists will give up easily when confronted with research dilemmas. Instead, I feel an obligation to state the obvious on this point just to put it out there just in case—if for no other reason than to "cover my bases."

Readers are right to note that above I've raised some questions concerning the manner in which institutions of higher learning work through—or don't work through—the nature and meaning of race and its tie to how particular populations experience life in the United States. I don't take any of that back, but I also want to suggest that there is something about higher education that might also help humanists develop a strategy for educating themselves regarding race and racism. No excuses, apply the same energy and effort to learning about race, racism, and white privilege as you do to other issues of societal concern.

Knowledge about how to read these materials, how to critically engage them, grows as a result of this process, and this growth positively influences how one moves through the world, which is the goal. Understanding how to approach material, however, is a challenge; but one for which I think there are strategies—good strategies—to employ. Books and related resources allow a certain productive vulnerability that exposes us, and in that moment of openness allows us to gain insight and rethink ourselves. This openness and this gaining of insight aren't certain, but I would argue they are difficult to achieve outside some version of this type of educational process. In short, *I'd suggest employing two strategies: engaged research and active learning.*

Let's take them in reverse. According to many experts, active learning is simply critical engagement with materials meant to push obligation onto those who are in the process of learning. That is to say, it requires those doing the reading, for example, to take responsibility for the process and outcomes. Institutions such as my own Rice University and Stanford University promote active learning as a vital means by which to approach education. I think the key is this: active learning as utilized at Rice, Stanford, and a variety of other institutions involves critical thinking about particular topics applied to resources such as books and then applied to actual situations. So, students—in this case humanists as students of race—gain knowledge that is refined through engagement with real-world situations and contexts. This is a shift in process in that it isn't a "banking model" of education: here's the information, now memorize it and move on. That banking model is in play when racial minorities are asked to teach—informally for the most part—whites about race. This can involve the side comment; the quick question about "your" people; the request for information that will explain their preconceived sense of racial minorities; or even the rehearsal of all the good that person has done to help "those" people. You get the idea, I'm sure. But, what I'm pointing to is a different process: gather materials; work through those materials; and apply those concepts to actual circumstances in the world. Sure, you might need to ask for suggestions—that's the key ask for a reading list, somewhere to start—but don't ask racial minorities to give you a short-course on race and racism. Get the materials, and do the work. Don't sidestep responsibility for informing yourself concerning the way race functions within the country you call "home." Don't ask someone else to do your work for you. This isn't really a matter of the "each one teach one" philosophy. Instead, it's more along the lines of get your resources together, buckle down, learn, and then apply within your context what you've learned. But again, this application should be guided—to the extent possible based on your location—by members of the community most profoundly affected by the issues of race you seek to address. Learning about race and white privilege becomes the necessary background for being mindful of the inner workings of racial dynamics and then doing the work well—or as well as possible.

What I am proposing isn't simply reading books. Sure, that's part of the process, but I'm also proposing another step: *active learning*. In short, useful attention to race/racism on the part of humanists requires *active and proactive learning*. That is to say, this process of knowledge development can't involve simply sitting and memorizing facts, or letting ideas flow over one. Required is a more proactive relationship to materials that involves a rather aggressive engagement, as if you were in direct contact with the author(s)—asking questions, probing for more meaning, and pushing for greater understanding. Don't just look at the words on the page, perhaps memorizing a few for quick quotations during gatherings. Instead, interrogate the text, pull it apart, and uncover its intent as well as its meaning. Then apply what you've uncovered. You can't be gentle in studying up on race and racism; be proactive when thinking and learning about it. More is gained this way, and racial minorities will note your seriousness, which will allow for more productive interactions across racial lines.

Humanists often do this implicitly with respect to issues more commonly recognized as of importance to humanist organizations and communities; but this doesn't always extend to those issues more debatable as central to humanism as a philosophy of life. They engage materials and pull them into their lived context; they share and discuss materials; and they apply critical-thinking skills to this full process. There's little whining about the difficulty of weeding through scientific materials, nor is there typically significant claiming of ignorance as a way to short-circuit the hard work of learning about scientific developments. There's an assumption this material is important and so people dig in. Sure, there's a general privileging of STEM (Science, Technology, Engineering, and Mathematics disciplines) in public speak about education; however, attention to race and its consequences demands recognition of the cultural matrix within the context of which our collective life takes place.

This work could involve moving through case studies during book club meetings, for instance—anything that allows one to take responsibility for learning. And, humanist organizations and other formal groupings of humanists might consider making such learning intrinsic to their missions, lodged in the organizational goals and objectives. In this way, the success of the organization—or whatever the formal gatherings are named—is tied to its growth with respect to issues of race. Reaching this point, this stage at which productive attention to race is fundamental, takes time and work. It isn't easy, but why should we assume it would be?

The United States, in part, has involved an experiment in racial differentiation tied to opportunity. This experiment has gone on for a long time and can't be short-circuited with a few quick words, a few activities, and a bit of remorseful intentionality. I appreciate any eagerness, and restlessness regarding effort to tackle issues of race, but time is required. I don't mean to say this in a way that allows patience to slide into procrastination. No, I'm urging informed strategy that is about both the short and the long "game." It is learning in the form of what many educators have called "*engaged research.*"

This entails, as researchers at Harvard and elsewhere have pointed out, learning that is thought and done—that engages the brain and the body as both vital. This brings study and service together in really useful ways that force an engagement with the world, with increased sensitivity to the dynamics of the world and the stakes for all the players. What I'm arguing is that the best efforts to understand race, racism, and white privilege entail aggressive study and dynamic application. Here's what I'm suggesting:

1. *Recognize there is a knowledge-based problem to address—* accept the straightforward call regarding knowledge as essential

for a proper understanding of what race is and how it functions to circumscribe life options and opportunities.

2. *Secure materials*—tap Internet search engines, ask for recommendations, attend events, and gather resources that will allow you to better understand race.

3. *Read actively*—don't be passive. Read materials about race in a critical and engaged fashion—book clubs, individual reading—whatever approach works best for you. Treat materials on race with the same seriousness that marks so much of the humanist approach to science. In part this means recognizing the contribution of humanities and the social sciences to knowledge production.

4. *Engage*—pull this information on race into your world, allow it to influence and affect how you deal with real-world situations. Don't keep it on an abstract level, but apply what you learn.

5. *Reevaluate*—learn from what you've encountered. Make applicable changes to your thinking and activities in light of what you've uncovered concerning the workings of race. This requires a bit of patience but not complacency. The tenacious nature of racial injustice isn't grounds for apathy nor surrender.

6. *Start the process over*—who hasn't heard the saying "be a life-long learner"? Need more be said? Racism and white privilege are tenacious and deeply embedded, so this isn't a read one text and then you are done kind of situation. Keep at it.

To recap: really look, listen, and explore—that is to say, study in a way that doesn't render you devoid of responsibility and accountability. Study in a way that pulls you into the workings of race. See how, where, and why you participate in the racial dynamics that define the United States. Engage. This is an important "to do" for humanists. It is true that humanists are all about information, about knowledge, and critical thinking based on reason and logic. That commitment to knowing, to really knowing, should inform *the* humanist take on race as well. Some might object to the definite article "the" in that last sentence, preferring to allow for more than one type of humanism accountable for more than one agenda. My use of that article, some might argue, is too limiting—making possible only a limited range of options and as a consequence restricting which persons can rightly claim the label "humanist." Despite such arguments, I want to keep that definite article in place, not simply because I'm stubborn, but rather because it serves an important function in terms of clarity of commitment. I'm one willing to argue that attention to issues of race should be present within the ethical work of any humanist organization and should be a point of concern for any humanist. How this ethical commitment is verbalized and acted out will vary across the geographies of life in the United States. Nonetheless, I'm convinced it ought to be a thread of continuity across the various pockets of humanism marking communities across the United States.

The term humanism might connote a variety of things with respect to definitions offered for it over the course of time. Some might argue it is simply the "human as the measure of all things." The American Humanist Association and related organizations connect that philosophy of life to logic, reason, rejection of supernaturalism, and a commitment to human activity in the world. The exact words used by the American Humanist Association are these: "Humanism is a progressive philosophy of life that, without theism and other supernatural beliefs, affirms our ability and responsibility to lead ethical lives of personal fulfillment that aspire to the greater good of humanity." I highlight this phrase from the definition—"lead ethical lives . . ." It is this last component that triggers my commitment to "the" humanist take on race. It isn't the definition of the concept that demands informed attention to race but rather it is the ethics that flows from and informs that perception of humanism that matters here. Humanism is a philosophy of life with what should be clear ethical and moral commitments shared across contexts, and I see no need and no use in excluding attention to race from this list of "ought" propositions promoted by this commitment to leading "ethical lives."

In the United States—in light of the significance race holds in terms of quality (and length) of life—humanism that doesn't address issues of race as one of its major commitments to justice is lacking. This isn't to exclude issues such as gender bias, classism, and so on. Rather it is to say racial justice needs to receive attention if the humans in humanism are to thrive.

So, yes, I would argue for "*the*" humanist commitment to informed, passionate, and engaged attention to issues of race as a fundamental and intrinsic dimension of what it means to be a humanist.

I understand the need to contextualize this ethical conduct in response to racial injustices as they are expressed in particular locations. However, this is not the same as to say a commitment to racial justice is an optional or debatable dimension of humanist identity and activity. That I cannot accept. From my vantage point to do humanism, to be a humanist, is to have a predisposition to conduct work to decrease racial bias and its consequences. Attention to racial injustice, for sure, isn't the full extent of the humanist agenda. I'm unable to accept arguments that it isn't an essential element of that agenda. Learning about the consequences of racial bias, I'm convinced, makes it difficult to see ending racism as a secondary element of humanist ethical action. So, to know, to really understand, racial discrimination is to seek its end.

To the extent sociocultural comfort is premised upon social and cultural codes that allow for racial discrimination, decreasing comfort might be thought of as a prerequisite for doing work toward racial justice. *One can't be comfortable and a catalyst for change.* If one were talking about exercise, one might say, "no pain, no gain." Although I'm not a proponent of redemptive suffering, I will say we have to be dislodged from our racial assumptions in order to promote better thinking. And this process isn't without its uneasiness. That is to say, if those with privilege are doing authentic racial justice work . . . it's going to be uncomfortable for them!

* * *

If You Want to Know More

As with the other chapters, here you'll find some additional materials for your consideration. Some of these materials deal with subjects quickly referenced in this chapter, but there are others that explore topics not addressed in this book. Together—those referenced and those not—they provide interesting food for thought.

Alexander, Michelle. *The New Jim Crow: Mass Incarceration in the Age of Colorblindness* (New York: The New Press, 2012).

Banaji, Mahzarin R. and Anthony G. Greenwald, *Blindspot: Hidden Biases of Good People* (New York: Delacorte Press, 2013).

Davis, Angela Y. *Freedom Is a Constant Struggle: Ferguson, Palestine, and the Foundations of a Movement* (New York: Haymarket Books, 2016).

Dewey, John. *Experience and Education* (New York: Free Press, 1997).

Eberhardt, Jennifer and Susan T. Fiske, editors. *Confronting Racism: The Problem and the Response* (Thousand Oaks, CA: Sage Publications, Inc., 1988).

Freire, Paulo. *Education for Critical Consciousness* (London: Bloomsbury, 2013).

Freire, Paulo. *Pedagogy of the Oppressed* (London: Bloomsbury Academic, 2000).

hooks, bell. *Killing Rage: Ending Racism* (New York: Holt Paperbacks, 1996).

hooks, bell. *Teaching to Transgress: Education as a Practice of Freedom* (New York: Routledge, 1994).

Irving, Debby. *Waking Up White, and Finding Myself in the Story of Race* (Chicago: Elephant Room Press, 2014).

Kivel, Paul. *Uprooting Racism: How White People Can Work for Racial Justice*, 3rd edition (Gabriola Island, BC: New Society Publishers, 2011).

Ross, Howard J. *Everyday Bias: Identifying and Navigating Unconscious Judgments in Our Daily Lives* (Lanham, MD: Rowman and Littlefield, 2014).

Simien, Justine. *Dear White People: A Guide to Inter-Racial Harmony in "Post-Racial" America* (New York: Atria, 2014).

Thandeka, *Learning to Be White: Money, Race, and God in America* (London: Bloomsbury Academic, 2000).

Walker, Alice. *Living by the Word: Selected Writings, 1973–1987* (New York: Mariner Books, 1989).

Wise, Tim. *Dear White America: Letter to a New Minority* (San Francisco: City Lights Publishers, 2012).

6

DIFFERENCE AS AN OPPORTUNITY

"More shades of the same" is a comforting strategy because it highlights the familiar while giving the pretense of difference. It's a natural but unproductive default position when race is the topic or the challenge.

The question: What kind of racial justice work might you find and promote, if difference is understood . . . differently?

* * *

Call it what you like: xenophobia, ethnocentrism, racism, nationalism, and the list goes on. What is important here is the underlying assumption and urge that motivates all of these various "-isms"— difference as a problem to solve.

For a very long time now, the United States has privileged sameness. Mild forms of this correspond to "melting pot" theories of culture and citizenship. These theories, in essence, promote the idea that people from across the globe have come to the United States and have been transformed into a unified population. In its less refined versions, this quest for sameness might take the form of pronouncements such as the familiar "Go back to their country," or "This is America . . . speak English!". Of course, there is rhetorical appeal to difference, but the bottom line has tended toward the fallback position: "Out of many, one." Check your dollar bills. Much older than the words "In God We Trust," introduced on bills in the

1950s as a response to the communist threat, is the coat of arms of the United States, which includes this phrase in Latin: "E Pluribus Unum." Even prior to the establishment of the United States, as colonists debated the merit of uniting with Great Britain or forging a truly independent nation, the idea of unity, of commonality, and of certain forms of sameness came into play. Thomas Paine feared destruction without the type of unity made possible through independence. In fact, he notes, "independence is the only bond that can tie and keep us together." Consider his words in *Common Sense* (1776), in support of this appeal to independence:

> The present state of America is truly alarming to every man who is capable of reflection. Without law, without government, without any other mode of power than what is founded on, and granted by courtesy. Held together by an unexampled concurrence of sentiment, which is nevertheless subject to change, and which every secret enemy is endeavoring to dissolve. Our present condition is, legislation without law; wisdom without a plan; a constitution without a name; and, what is strangely astonishing, perfect Independence contending for dependence.

I am not arguing the fine points or details of Paine's call for independence, nor am I providing a detailed analysis of *Common Sense*. My concern isn't his political philosophy per se, nor the arguments for or against the development of an independent nation able to hold its own in global economics. Nor am I concerned with his critique of religion as a guide for life, or his distinction between government and society—subjects that are beyond the scope of this particular volume. My goal is more focused, narrower than that. I am only pointing out the manner in which notions of difference, sameness, conformity, and unity ground earlier conversation in North America and pushed forward into the twenty-first century.

The idea that the United States is a collection of difference reduced to sameness is older than the assumption that belief in God is an appropriate statement for a secular nation's currency. Each in its own way—philosophically and theologically—is intended to submerge difference below a sea of shared knowledge meant to promote a common commitment that unifies by seeking to render any difference superficial enough to ignore if not wipeout. Opposition has been a problem to solve, a source of conflict and confusion easily lending itself to discord and destruction. Difference has been seen as a type of chaos, and chaos destroys; or, at least this is how the story has been told.

While for some this is a secular project, for many others it is a project with deep theological roots that wrap around biblically derived values and objectives giving them weight and meaning that extends beyond any particular moment in history. Think about the Bible as a type of fiction, which it is, a myth meant to say something about how strong community is formed and what serves to threaten it. The text is a celebration and warning regarding conformity and sameness. The writers of that book see both not as politically expedient (otherwise the Children of Israel might have had a different attitude toward the Egyptians, and the followers of Jesus against the Romans) but as metaphysically and theologically required for prosperity. In the biblical account of human development, this push for sameness, for commonality, isn't simply a matter of human psychology or emotional development. It isn't a strain of human evolution made necessary by chemical and biological determinations inevitable and biting.

The scientific impossibility of biblical stories matter little to its adherents, and what the Bible suggests concerning proper conduct and the limits of community is considered beyond question. From the very beginning of the Bible—or at least how it has been presented to readers—threat is present in the from of difference revolving around unwillingness to abide by regulations. In the Book of Genesis, Adam and Eve are kicked out the Garden of Eden as a consequence of attempting to be different. Nimrod is painted a villain because he challenges the normativity of divine dictates by promoting a different perception of human capacity and ability. He builds a tower that reaches the heavens, and the insecure superpower causes confusion—differences in language amongst humans—as a way of destroying their sense of creativity, capability, and hope. In important ways, the very story of the children of Israel is about conformity, about developing sameness over against cultural-religious difference (e.g., Egyptians, Moabites, Hittites, and Canaanites).

What were the faithful encouraged to believe resulted from this quest for a unified and unquestioned sameness and normativity? The answer is simple: happiness and success. Prosperity and power are tied to a cosmic standard of sameness and allegiance to the codes of that sameness. On the other hand, difference resulted in pain and suffering, and distance from the source of life (e.g., God).

A quest for sameness, the wiping out of difference, doesn't end with the Hebrew Bible. The New Testament promotes a similar sameness: the Children of Israel are the model, a somewhat flawed model, but the Jesus they rejected promotes a new type of sameness, a new challenge to difference as a problem to solve. New Testament unity is a sameness played out through an allegiance to Jesus' particular brand of theological-political and social thought. The difference to address and wipe out is religious traditions not in line with Jesus' teachings. And, the sameness desired is religious continuity through belief in Jesus as the "son" of "God." Over time there would develop some difference regarding the details of this commitment to Jesus, but overall there was a general and growing sense that "Jesus is the way, the truth and the light."

Pushing forward over a good number of centuries, many of those who made the journey to the "New World" bought into this story of sameness as divinely required. They borrowed the Christian Tradition and fancied themselves the "new" children of Israel, the ones God loves. The North American territory—with their imprint— was understood as a select location for God's people. And while there were differences (often fought with great energy and bloody violence) in the Christianity practiced, there was a sense that theism in general and Christianity in particular was the right life guide. Humans, as scriptures lamented, were a dangerous lot when operating on their own, and so it is only by means of cosmic restrictions worked out through theistic faith that humans can be saved from the chaos that is human nature. What makes all this work? According to the Christian tradition, it's the unmerited grace of the Divine. Faith in the power of accepting this grace promotes restricting of life along the lines of conformity to sameness that opens humans to the ultimate gift of "heaven."

This is a fantastic story—meant here as a negative, as a way of describing wild imagination—that points to the theologizing of sameness and the demonizing of difference as the glue that holds together the universe, or at least the United States. It is a story—a metanarrative—that is supported by what theologians and historians call "Manifest Destiny"—the assumption that the well-being and longevity of a people and nation is ordained by divine forces and, therefore, is certain. The success, in this case, of the United States and its racial policies is simply a historical manifestation of divine favor. In short, this success—tied to racial policies and a sense of sameness as vital to the integrity of the nation—is meant to be.

Conformity/sameness has cosmic design and purpose that drives it forward even as humanity resists the process—even when humans assume they actually have the final word on the development of the world. This is because there is always a remnant, a select group that maintains awareness of the divine demand for obedience, sameness, or conformity. There are always those who understand themselves as guardians of the "right way" even when those around them resist. This group understands history to be teleological in nature—that is to say, it has purpose and it moves toward its determined conclusion. Martin Luther King, Jr., for instance, gets to this point when arguing, "the arch of the moral universe is long but it bends toward justice." They, the guardians, perceive themselves as knowing and acting to safeguard the best way forward—which is typically the way things have always been done based on long-held beliefs. Others may not be aware of the danger at the "gates," so to speak, but these guardians know what's at stake and are prepared to do what they need to do so as to maintain security, peace, and sameness. Preserving or restoring the greatness of the nation is their agenda, and this often means assimilating difference or destroying difference that can't be massaged into sameness. In either case, a nation built on the rightness of whiteness undergirds what takes place over the course of the centuries marking the emergence, refinement, and perpetuation of the "American way of life" against all foes (internal and external).

This being the case, humanists, atheists, and other nontheists from before the formal development of the nation were suspect and assumed to represent a difference with limited value, if any lasting value at all. Their disbelief might bring the wrath of God and as a consequence the destruction of society. From the perspective of theists making this argument, the examples of this happening were plenty and there was no real reason to take a chance on destruction. The type of suffering God's displeasure entails wasn't temporary; God held a grudge, and theists don't want to run the risk. Keep in mind the words of one of the most in/famous colonial preachers, Jonathan Edwards, whose well-known sermon from 1741 bore this title: "Sinners in the Hands of an Angry God." That, and the tragic story he told in that sermon, was enough to keep lots of people in line, and similar theological scare tactics continued. I can't resist sharing some of the words from that sermon:

> The use of this awful subject may be for awakening unconverted persons in this congregation. This you have heard is the case of every one of you that are without Christ. That world of misery, that lake of burning fire, is stretched out wide under you. There is the dreadful pit of the glowing flames of the wrath of God; there is hell's wide gaping mouth open; and you have nothing to stand upon, nor anything to take hold of; there is nothing between you and hell but the air; it is only the power and mere pleasure of God that holds you up.

Damn! There's nothing subtle about this message of conformity or else. What Edwards proposes involves difference based on the biblically supported and preached notion that disbelief could result in the colonies, then nation, losing its privileged position and the resulting physical and psychological goods that went along with the security associated with that posture toward life in the world. Confine oneself to the moral vision and ethical conduct outlined in the Bible, or suffer the consequences. It's a rigid life, but, according to Edwards, the alternative is dire. As many readers will know from lived experience, this disregard for the difference constituted by disbelief continues to mark the United States despite the growing number of those who reject theism in its various forms. Great figures have rejected Christianity as a proper marker of political life and cultural sameness to be embraced. Even these figures, such as the oft-noted Thomas Jefferson, tended to appreciate the need to control for racial difference as a way to safeguard the normativity of sameness represented by whiteness. For instance, a common example of this: the founding documents marking out the experiment of Democracy called the United States had no intention to include people of African descent in the workings and rights of that nation. Having taken land and worked (not always consciously but effectively nonetheless) to destroy cultures already present, the emerging nation assumed any allegiance to "foreign" entities or ideals would only compromise the security of the "United States."

Certain modes of sameness have been challenged (e.g., theism as the basic posture of the nation and the bible as an essential guide), but others that also serve to shape life in the United States have been embraced and written into the meta-narrative of the United States and its "people." And various rules and regulations, practices and warnings were put in place to safeguard against potential threats—"domestic and foreign." Humanists and theists, while disagreeing on the unifying nature of shared religious belief, have tended to accept at least passively other ways of thinking about difference as a problem preferring to remain warm and comfortable in a cocoon of commonality. Humanists fight against a particular metaphysics that assumes anything supernatural and transhistorical in nature, but don't fight so hard against theories of political life that assume the necessary integrity of the nation/state—the "special" quality of democracy represented by the United States. This assumption of specialness ties to a challenging of any approach, any policy or practice, troubling this sense of stability. Sometimes it's expressed this way: "Sure, we have problems in our country, but it's a better situation than anywhere else in the world." Difference here is a political problem that cuts against the purpose of the nation-state—damaging its significance, longevity, and destiny. "Tradition"—whether in politics, economics, social dynamics, or another sphere of human interaction—becomes code for sameness over against difference and change. It, tradition, is a static memory meant to foster conformity.

Religion isn't the only cultural construction that plays on tradition as a way of fighting off questions and critique. Think in terms of more secular practices and ideas repeated over time so often that they just "are" and few question their relevance: "These beliefs on difference exist, so they must have importance or we wouldn't hold to them anymore . . . right?" Consider, for example, the practice of saluting the flag, and standing for and repeating the Pledge of Allegiance. Whether or not one throws in the "under God" or not, the words and actions constitute a tradition—a practice solidified as part of the collective consciousness—that marks out something of what it means to be "an American." Those who fail to mimic the postures and wording of this tradition run the risk of dirty looks, rude gestures, or worse. This response takes a variety of forms depending on location, context, and intensity of the assumed offense to the "American way."

I highlight a particular arrangement of racism here, but there is also xenophobia for instance. Both—racism and xenophobia—entail disregard and fear of difference as a negative and as a troubling reality tied to the "look" of the body. Both are tied to the manner in which the United States understands and speaks about itself. While the former—racism—as it is discussed typically involves a threat from within, xenophobia is about an effort to avoid this situation of an internal threat by highlighting the danger of foreigners infiltrating and not assimilating. "Speak English!" "Why do you wear those weird outfits, and why do women in your community cover like that . . . it's a problem." These are just a few of the statements that speak to this demand for sameness and the ways in which this demand can be psychologically and emotionally, if not physically, violent. Such responses also point to the manner in which this fear of difference in the form of the "alien"—defined in terms of culture, social constructs, and so on—involves a forgetfulness in that it fails to recognize those who claim the United States as "home" come from ancestors who were themselves foreigners.

These responses to difference derive from a deep fear that nonconformity pulls at the social fabric—the delicate connective tissue—that holds together these *United* States. Difference, hence, is believed to damage the ability of the nation to preserve its sociopolitical and cultural integrity. In this restrictive thinking is an assumption that a clear litmus test of belonging exists and can be easily and quickly applied: Does the person look "American"? Does the person speak "American"? Does the person's aesthetic suggest "American-ness"? Do the person's political allegiances suggest a commitment to the "American" way of life?

These questions are often asked in a crude manner. But, I would argue, this isn't the case with most humanists; yet, there remains a similar logic even for more refined humanists. Even for these enlightened folks, it isn't uncommon for there to be in place the logic that difference is a problem to solve. It's a more nuanced and less rhetorically violent sense of sameness as normative, but the outcome is similar. Sameness is the American way. Both theists and humanists make at least implicit claims that what it means to be an "American," to rightly live and benefit from the United States, can be easily deciphered and this happens in a way that privileges whiteness.

What I offer here isn't a full investigation of the complexities of racism as a disregard for difference. Rather, this discussion is meant to simply point out the problematic nature of ways of thinking and behaving that restrict creativity and opportunities based on a false sense of entitlement forged by reducing diversity and difference. In a word, "I'll make you like me . . . and you'll like it, trust me."

Initially it was easier to address difference. For example, the "first nation" populations—the American Indians—were geographically restricted and when possible impressionable members of those populations were coerced and brainwashed into an embrace of Europeans sensibilities. They were taken from family, educated into the assumptions of European superiority, dressed like Europeans, trained to speak and think like Europeans—all meant to make their physical features less pronounced and their commitment to the markers of commonality and sameness—e.g., "whiteness"—more apparent. Thus, the systemic workings of sameness were rescued from the threat of cultural difference. The African population had its very humanity challenged and was dealt with through legal structures that positioned them as property and that didn't really question the integrity of "sameness." And, when this integrity was challenged eventually on a small or large scale, difference was addressed through cultural manipulation (e.g., stereotypes) and violence (e.g., beatings and lynching)—anything to get back to the "good old days" when the normativity of a white standard of life went without serious question and without substantive pushback. In many instances, sex became a tool of cultural manipulation in that these "foreign" populations could be altered through sex. The rape of enslaved Africans is just one instance of this alternate use of power to maintain the significance of commonality.

Some Europeans posed a problem along the lines of ethnic difference, but even this could be addressed through a general category of whiteness earned (e.g., by mimicking the practices and language of whiteness) or purchased in a variety of ways (e.g., like using economic success to secure social mobility and new cultural contexts). I think the ability to "perform" whiteness, for instance, by the Irish—who early on were viewed as of little more significance than African Americans—is some of what's meant by racial minorities being told they "are acting white."

All in all, difference could be addressed and managed as a virus of sorts with commonality or sameness as the treatment. This wasn't a reasonable argument being made really, but rather it was a gut reaction that confronted reason and altered it to fit the needs of fear and anxiety. The call for conformity is driven by and feeds from an ever-present quantity of "what ifs." What if "those people" take over? What if "those people" move into my neighborhood? What if "those people" force their culture on us "Americans"? The list goes on and attacks *ad hominem*.

On this score, small aesthetic differences could trigger strong reaction. Think, for example, of "zoot suits"—a long coat with exaggerated shoulders and bagging high-waist pants that narrowed dramatically near the ankle. They were fashionable with African American, Chicanos, and Italian Americans during the 1940s. However, this style of dress marked difference on the level of aesthetics that pushed against the assumed "look" of American life. Nonetheless, for these young men this style difference was a soft way of speaking to value and worth outside the confines of U.S. conformity. It was a way of presenting themselves, making themselves visible and claiming "space." They marked their difference with pride and flair as a way of speaking the truth of their significance and importance—their rightful occupation of time and space. They highlighted their bodies and gave them aesthetic appeal within their own circles of influence and they cared little how others might think about their clothing selections. Their "outsider" style status highlighted their difference in the face of a quest for sameness. This aesthetic offense was countered by violence against them in many instances. These suits were banned during World War II and one can imagine this had something to do with the manner in which war spurs a desire for unity, for sameness. One couldn't "rally around the flag" with an exaggerated coat and high-waist baggy pants! For instance, attacks on Mexican American young people in 1943, given the name the "zoot suit war," were in part because the zoot suit marked them unpatriotic.

What I offer here is a condensed and spotty discussion of a rather intense period, but even this quick reference points to the way in which markers of difference—even dress—can trigger a violent push for sameness under the guise of protecting the nation from destruction by an internal enemy.

This violence (in a variety of forms) is the easy move, the easy approach to the complex nature of our collective life that requires little of us and gives us little in return. It is a move driven by a type of sensory deprivation by which our ability to note layered realities is compromised, and exposure to this complexity causes a reaction that "feels" like an embodied pressure and pain that threatens everything that matters. Life, as it is expected to play, is challenged. In this way, difference is perceived as a disruption. This call for conformity has made "us" creatures of habit opposed to anything that pushes against the old reliable comfort zone of "sameness." And, this fall back position of sameness urges resentment toward those who push against uniformity.

Embedded in this mindset is the assumption of protection, or a sense of safety in sameness and threat in difference. If we can only keep things the way they are, goes the logic, then we can prevent destruction and maintain what is best about this nation. If we can safeguard against change, we can remain firm in convictions of special status and importance, which are firm and longstanding.

Uncertainty. Change is difficult for most; it breaks rhythm and requires rethinking and reassessment, which includes some version of this question: What's wrong with my activities, and me, if I now need to change? Have I been wrong this whole time? If my thinking and doing are wrong, then I am wrong . . .?

A study published in the November 2010 issue of *Journal of Experimental Social Psychology* by Scott Eidelman et al. notes that there is a direct relationship between how long an idea or practice has been around and the value people subscribe to it. The longer its existence, the more people value it and assume it is important, right, and meant to be kept around. As a variety of others have noted over the years, including Dr. Heidi Grant Halvorson in a January 2012 post on the *Huffington Post* titled "Explained: Why We Don't Like Change," this bias toward length of existence as a measure of value can be changed. Yes, it is possible for people to push beyond this way of thinking, which is a way of thinking that can support some really problematic behaviors and thought patterns. But, it is important first to recognize that this bias is in place and that it isn't something hardwired into us. It can be addressed, dismantled, and new patterns of thinking and doing can be put in its place. In this case, racial difference as a problem to solve can be replaced with a more healthy and potentially richer approach.

In all fairness, humanists have acknowledged difference, but as an opportunity to reassert some type of normative behavior, look, attitude, and so on. This approach produces more shades of the same—African Americans, Latinos/as, Asian Americans, and so on, appreciated to the extent they model the social norms and regulations preferred by the dominant population. And, success in this regard is often attested to through remarks like, "You aren't like the others . . ." In some cases, the desire to wipe out difference takes the form of a fog of help: "I am committed to social justice, and I have always given of myself to the struggle. But people [read: some particular racial minority population] don't appreciate my efforts." This, on its face, doesn't seem harmful. In fact, again on the surface, it seems to suggest the right attitude. But here's how difference is damaged even in this scenario: the "look" of progress, the litmus test of advancement, isn't determined by those who most widely suffer from racial injustice. To the contrary, the attitude of white "partners" remains focused on how whites feel about the situation, and what white Americans understand as acceptable change and important benchmarks of success.

Sameness in this situation is framed by what makes white Americans comfortable. Every group has this burden; yet, white Americans determining the proper benchmarks of progress, and the cartography of racial advancement, will mean undoubtedly participation in the world along the lines of the dominant populations sensibilities and sensitivities. That is to say, this call for sameness means racial minorities must continue to tiptoe around white American idiosyncrasies.

I'm not suggesting there is always something malicious about this posture toward difference. No, some who hold to it are genuinely concerned with justice and social transformation. However, difference as a problem limits the ways in which social transformation can be mapped out because it maintains problematic conventions concerning race that keep white privilege in place by pushing racial minorities to be more like the "white" population. Again, the off-putting so-called compliments: "You're not like the others," or "You are a credit to your race" all play off this underlying convention regarding difference as best addressed through a demand for sameness.

This brings us back to "E Pluribus Unum" . . . or something along those lines—back to the urge for continuity of thought, practice, perception, and being—back to sameness that wipes out racial difference and in its place installs whiteness as ultimate authority. The genius of this process revolves around the ways in which this "white" washing (pun intended) of difference is assumed natural, the way things should (no, *must*) be if society is to thrive and be all it has the capacity to be now and always.

As should be clear at this point, race difference as a problem to solve is old, very old, in the United States. Albeit embedded in the

American popular imagination, it can be addressed. The related dynamics can't be changed in such a way as to control the impulse to wipe out racial difference. The psychological supports for this dislike for difference are tenacious but they can be altered, and the material and physical ramifications of this push against difference can also be exposed and resisted through justice work.

It's important to keep in mind that being reminded of this preference for sameness *isn't* the same as being called a racist. There may be a connection between the two to the extent racism becomes a tool by means of which sameness is preserved. This, however, isn't to say preference for sameness is always acted out in ways that dimensions the well-being of others. This demand for the elimination of difference is a failure of vision and deprivation in that it amounts to people seeing things from a limited and limiting vantage point. Still I don't want to be understood as offering a justification for this push toward sameness in its various forms. **It, let me be clear, is a bad thing.** So, to the contrary, it should be resisted and fought. The link between racism and a push toward sameness is a caution. It is a reminder that this urge toward sameness can have bad consequences for racial minorities and this recognition by white Americans (and racial minorities) might be uncomfortable *but* required. Still, keep in mind, however, the bad consequences aren't just for racial minorities. To think so is to reenforce the normativity of whiteness. Everyone pays a high price; everyone loses when sameness is pushed in that the possibilities for our collective life are reduced for all. Everyone suffers. Every U.S. citizen, then, lives in a society without great imagination, without strong creativity, where embrace of risk is a prerequisite for success sufficient to make a dent in the structures of racial injustice.

So, I prefer to think of difference as an opportunity, as a chance to add complexity to community and to learn from approaches and perspectives outside what is considered normative. It is to be open to other viewpoints and perspectives, to learn from what is unfamiliar and disliked. At its core, isn't this approach constitutive of democracy at its best? Difference offers a chance to stretch intellectually, psychologically, emotionally, and in other ways that open new avenues of advancement. It's an opportunity to appreciate what has been marginal to U.S. life and understand its actual centrality. Put a different way, complexity and diversity have always anchored life in the United States, despite the fact this has been covered at times and denied at other historical moments. We just haven't always recognized this fact. In a certain way, difference as opportunity points to the need to appreciate cultural diversity, learn from it, and embrace possibilities that push us beyond the familiar and comfortable. This take on difference involves some risk to the extent it pushes us into the unfamiliar; but, there is something of real value in pushing ourselves to step outside the box, to use a tired metaphor.

There are steps that can be taken to rethink difference in more positive ways. I suggest only a few here:

1. Whether one initially embraced difference as a negative or not isn't the root issue. It is important to recognize problematizing difference as a limited/limiting way of thinking that is deeply embedded in the narrative of American life.

2. The argument by some that a fear of difference might be "natural" doesn't make it necessary, so it should and can be addressed and changed. The impulse to wipe out difference is an impulse that needs to be acknowledged and controlled.

3. Recognize that the popular narrative of the nation is based on bad history in that it fails to recognize that difference is in the nation's DNA.

4. Come to grips with the need to wipe out any sense that the United States is special and that its cultural boundaries can be anything other than porous.

5. Understand that effort to wipe out difference has meant numerous forms of violence against people, and that change will require dismantling social structures and practices that paint difference as the enemy as opposed to seeing the effort to normalize whiteness as the problem to address.

6. Be open to the idea that difference allows for new ways of thinking and doing that are complex and creative.

7. The more the better. Solidarity is a good basis from which to work in that it doesn't seek to wipe out difference but rather to promote communication and action that draws wisdom and strength from difference.

8. Recognize tension and paradox can be productive and can serve to undergird constructive thinking and doing. That is to say, the goal should be working with difference in ways that allow diversity to become a source of connection.

9. As is the case with many of the other recommendations in this book, it is important to recognize rethinking difference will produce some discomfort and disorientation.

* * *

If You Want to Know More

As with the other chapters, I offer some materials for those who are interested in gaining more perspective, context, and content than is available in this chapter.

Austin, Algemon, *America Is Not Post-Racial: Xenophobia, Islamophobia, Racism, and the 44th President* (Santa Barbara, CA: Praeger, 2015).

Coulthard, Glen Sean. *Red Skin, White Masks: Rejecting the Colonial Politics of Recognition* (Minneapolis, MN: University of Minnesota Press, 2014).

Fanon, Frantz, *Black Skin, White Masks* (New York: Grove, 2008).

Fanon, Frantz, *Wretched of the Earth* (New York: Grove, 2005).

Goldstein, Alyosha, editor. *Formations of United States Colonialism* (Durham, NC: Duke University Press, 2014).

Healey, Joseph F. *Diversity and Society: Race, Ethnicity, and Gender* (Thousand Oaks, CA: Sage, 2013).

Hsu, Madeline Y. *The Good Immigrants: How the Yellow Peril Became the Model Minority* (Princeton, NJ: Princeton University Press, 2015).

Muhammad, Khalil Gibran. *The Condemnation of Blackness: Race, Crime, and the Making of Modern Urban America* (Cambridge, MA: Harvard University Press, 2011).

Pagan, Eduardo Obregon. *Murder at Sleepy Lagoon: Zoot Suits, Race, and Riots in Wartime LA* (Chapel Hill, NC: University of North Carolina, 2003).

Roediger, David R. *Working Toward Whiteness: How America's Immigrants Became White: The Strange Journey from Ellis Island to the Suburbs* (New York: Basic Books, 2006).

Romero, R. Todd. *Making War and Minting Christians: Masculinity, Religion, and Colonialism in Early New England* (Amherst, MA: University of Massachusetts Press, 2011).

Tchen, John Kuo Wei. *Yellow Peril!: An Archive of Anti-Asian Fear* (New York: Verso, 2014).

Wistrich, Robert S. *Demonizing the Other: Antisemitism, Racism, and Xenophobia* (New York: Routledge, 1999).

7

LEARNING FROM "UNLIKELY" SOURCES

I don't know anything about hip hop culture. It seems so violent. Why are they so angry and so materialistic? Those are common questions, but there's a better one humanists should ask: what can we learn from hip hop culture?

* * *

We humanists have made our presence felt. Often our rhetoric is self-assured, and vividly displayed is our willingness to confront the theism-bias embedded in the workings of the United States. Despite all this, humanist activities still appear entrenched in an apologetic mode—a significant expenditure of resources meant to say, "We are here and, by the way, we are good people." Even more aggressive forms of humanist engagement, those meant to challenge the religious and convert them through strong confrontation and mockery, from my perspective, betray the same apologetic tone. Neither what some derogatorily call a conformist approach (i.e., accommodations) nor the more self-righteous confrontational approach provides a sufficiently constructive and robust depiction of what humanistic orientations promote. This type of posture toward work doesn't allow for the accomplishment of a full agenda to diminish the theism-centered discourse (and structures of interaction) guiding so many dimensions of public life. And this is because humanists are still playing by the rules offered by theists. That is to say, there is embedded in humanist approaches an effort to get theists to appreciate (perhaps even like?) humanists. But why worry about that? Furthermore, is this type of regard even achievable?

It can still be problematic to embrace publicly humanism. Yet a typical approach to this situation does little to change this dilemma in that humanists' marginality is embedded in the rhetoric of the nation—and has become tragically the grammar of the public sphere—and guided by the temperament of the uninformed. Even if this weren't the case, being liked hasn't done much to change the outlook for other marginalized groups. What it can produce is paternalism, patronizing attitudes that actually stymie advancement and inclusion. Perhaps humanists might aim to be disliked but respected? Yet, what does being respected entail for humanists? What's the look, the texture, of this respect and what does securing and keeping it require of them?

Needed at this point is more attention to the construction of an alternate grammar of life along with new modalities of ethical/moral insight and practice that speak to the benefits of humanistic thinking and doing. Humanists have demonstrated some creativity in generating this message, but still seem a bit stuck and in need of inspiration. Mindful of this, this chapter proposes a source of assistance worthy of consideration—hip hop culture.

What I have in mind extends beyond an appreciation for the outstanding work of humanist hip hop artists, and instead includes attention to the pedagogical possibilities offered by the larger cultural movement. So, no need to worry; I'm not asking readers to turn their baseball caps backward, or forget about their sensible shoes and conservative clothing choices. I'm not calling on humanists to become hip hop advocates or fans. Rather, I am suggesting that hip hop provides a particularly compelling heuristic, or in other words it offers a model. My aim is to encourage recognition of hip hop as an interpretative tool by means of which humanists might learn how to better do what they say humanism is all about—and to do so in ways that appreciate the creativity lodged in our relative marginality and despised status.

A link between humanism and hip hop is not as absurd as one might initially think, not when one considers a common knowledge root marking much of the thinking undergirding both. That is to say, both humanistic sensibilities and hip hop culture share a human-centered and earthly sense of what the human is; both stem (although there are nuances to this) from a similar perception of evidence-based free thought and a signifying of supernatural claims and transhistorical assertions. Furthermore, in U.S. culture, both humanists and members of the hip hop community are labeled marginal and problematic figures whose activities/beliefs fly in the face of normative moral and ethical structures of life.

I propose an embrace of this connection and attention to what can be learned from the successes of hip hop culture. While it has its problematic dimensions—elements of violence, homophobia, misguided materialism, and so on borrowed from the storehouse of American culture—there are ways in which this cultural force has offered important challenges to the "American way of life." It has outlived calls for its demise and pronouncements of its fad-like quality. Even those who fear or dislike hip hop have been forced to recognize it and address life in this historical moment in light of it.

Lodged within the decaying infrastructure of urban life in New York City during the late 1970s, hip hop culture—the music, aesthetic, dance, and visual art known as tagging and graffiti—provided a mode of communication and exchange for typically disenfranchised young people.

Hip hop is not the first cultural form to wrestle with the difficulties and limits marking the (post)modern period—i.e., the period of history beginning with industrial decline and the Second World War. Yet, it does so with a type of rawness and through imaginaries that push thought about and experience of the world beyond affected representations. The traumas and angst of the world are expressed in graphic form. In certain ways, hip hop culture offers a new language, an alternate grammar and vocabulary for articulating the nature and meaning of life. In other words, the various genres of rap—what might be described as status rap, socially conscious rap, and gangsta rap—offer perspectives on this basic arrangement: how does one make life meaningful within the context of an absurd world? Within rap music there are strong representations of this absurdity, with perhaps the most compelling being death. Humanists are well aware of death; they know the science behind it, and are quite reasonable and logical with respect to it. Yet, humanists live in cultural worlds that are not fully explained by means of scientific formulas. Living toward death requires a particular cartography, a peculiar mapping of existence that marks out the cultural contours of humans being humans. And for this, humanists should turn to hip hop in that there are ways in which it promotes significant attention to the tensions and paradox associated with efforts to map out life structures within a context marked by the look, feel, and smell of death. It offers a compelling way of describing and addressing the grotesque dimensions of human demise much too graphic for most polite, humanist conversations.

Through a creative signifying of dominant strategies for life and more graphic modes of expressing life meaning within the context of absurdity of our world as we encounter it, hip hop marks a demand for visibility in a world more comfortable with invisibility. It has offered a way of speaking about and speaking to the tragic nature of human existence, without surrender to the nihilism theistic intellectuals like Cornel West fear. Instead, it provides comfort with paradox and an imagining of marginality as place for transformation.

Whereas hip hop has turned status as a despised and troubling but short-term fad into a powerful tool for shaping cultural worlds across a global geography, humanist movements have not been as fortunate in their effort to create status and more transnational influence.

Humanists are trying to fix this situation through public conversation and praxis, and through organizational infrastructure expanding beyond North America. However, there is a flaw in this approach in that such effort tends to involve strategies tied (at least loosely) to the methods and logic associated with the civil rights movement of the mid-twentieth century. These methods and this logic require acceptance of an assumption that moral outrage made visible constitutes the means for advancement. There is in this arrangement belief that progress is somehow linear and human history purpose driven. I am not pushing for rejection of the civil rights movement and, of course, humanists aren't alone in appealing for inspiration to this process and this particular moment of struggle. After all, some important shifts in policy resulted from that movement. Yet, there are ways in which appeal to mid-twentieth-century techniques may not be the best strategy for the godless. For instance, popular imagination around the civil rights movement is overwhelmingly (but not of necessity) connected to a romanticizing of certain communities of struggle—e.g., churches. And the rhetoric used to articulate that civil right struggle draws from the language of those particular communities. In addition, left in place after the civil rights movement is an ethical posture toward the world based on a privileging of supernatural claims/assumptions, a spiritual sense of the human's place in the world, as well as an accompanying sense of sanctity afforded theism that humanists fight. Why maintain an approach to transformation of thought and quality of life that historically has privileged some of the very things humanists hope to eliminate?

Instead, humanists might take seriously as a source of information and strategy the best of hip hop's framing of and posture toward sociocultural and political struggle—and in this case, racial justice. And, this process might begin with several considerations related to a humanist posture toward the nature and meaning of the humanist movement as well as its self-understanding and its work. I'd like to offer these examples of this rethinking.

1. "Thick" Diversity

Hip hop culture has demonstrated an impressive ability to trouble rigid cultural boundaries of nation-states and in this way promote diversity of expression, opinion, and so on. To speak of hip hop is to mention an array of racial and ethnic groups—each with celebrated contributions to its development. There is a depth and thickness to diversity as modeled by hip hop culture—despite some of its shortcomings. Again I want to make certain this discussion is connected in the mind of the reader to the discussion within earlier chapters, particularly the last one. So, while reading, please keep in mind the discussion of difference and associated challenges from the previous chapter.

Humanists voice an interest in diversity—and in certain awkward ways hope to promote it—but such efforts tend to produce what I will call *performative diversity*. By this I mean symbolic appreciation for "difference" as a marker of strength. It produces more *visible* "minority" communities of humanists, but this does little to change decision-making and the array of concerns promoted within these movements, and how these concerns are arranged and ranked. Yet, as hip hop culture has demonstrated, more substantive diversity requires production of an organic system of symbols and signs that draw from the sensibilities of a wide-ranging group of participants. Adherents, so to speak, have to see themselves reflected in the workings of movements, see themselves as having real potential for involvement (e.g., leadership positions that shape the form and content of movements), and see the humanist movement lexicon reflect their language of life. So, what is required involves the development of descriptions of racialized life and its corrections that pull from the experiences of people—that speak to and from the lives of people. I'm not suggesting humanists and others should simply use the language of hip hop culture. Rather, I'm suggesting it's time to learn a lesson from hip hop concerning the development of language that captures graphically the conditions of life as we encounter them and that offers a way forward true to our circumstances, resources, and skills. White Americans working toward racial justice in their contexts, for instance, need to speak in ways that reflect the complexity and urgency of current circumstances and that demonstrate respect for those most deeply impacted by racial dynamics. In part this involves a push against abstract descriptions, and a call for more "earthly" linguistic engagements with life.

In some cases, direct engagement has increased humanist numbers; however, the assumption that such tactics work in every context is a type of arrogance and disregard for cultural nuance. Not many African Americans, for example, leave churches because of direct confrontation. To think so shows ignorance concerning the late twentieth-century patterns of growth for black churches—patterns that have little to do with theological commitment and more to do with networking opportunities and cultural connections. Simply denouncing and ridiculing Christian theology and belief does little to persuade: what do humanists offer as alternate sources of networking and cultural community? The assumption reason can trump theology also fails to recognize the manner in which theology mutates and theism (e.g., Christian churches) transforms itself. Its contemporary manifestations are less rigid than the pre-Enlightenment theologizing humanists tend to target in their critiques. Talk of the end of religion also fails to acknowledge regional differences, and ignores new (and successful) religious formulations such as the Prosperity Gospel and the mega-churches adhering to it. These churches do not fall victim to typical critiques in that the most glaring examples of bad thinking are softened, and instead they highlight the Bible as a tool for advancing one's economic goals.

Theism is flexible, and does not die easy. While attempting to dismantle it, humanists must also recognize the short-term need to work in ways to lessen the negative impact it has on quality of life. If readers think I'm wrong, think again. The "look" of the typical humanistic gathering and the perpetual asking of the "how do we recruit people of color" questions do more than suggest I'm right.

Deconstruction of theism's flaws is required, but that must be followed by constructive projects and conversations that actually offer alternatives. Smash the idols, but replace them with deeply human and compelling meaning-making opportunities and platforms.

Humanist approaches have suffered from an underlying assumption that there is one way to promote humanism, but this is wrong because people are messy, and communities are difficult to capture. And so, humanists should think in terms of multiple approaches to our work—an array of strategies that mirror the complexities of our social arrangements. Thinking this way and acting in light of such a philosophy of engagement might also cut down on the amount of infighting humanists experience on occasion. But again, this requires an organic language—a vocabulary and grammar robust and descriptive enough to capture the imagination of humanists across various lines of tactical difference and constructive enough to translate to those outside our groups.

2. Significance of the Ordinary

As I have written elsewhere, such as in my book *The End of God Talk* (2012), it is often the case that humanists, in order to expand their presence and counter the foolishness of theistic orientations, highlight the unusual, the atypical and grand figures and moments within the history of our movement. Or, when the ordinary is highlighted it is juxtaposed to what they consider the markers of greatness. I would suggest such a move does not serve humanists well. Instead, humanists should give more attention to the significance, the invaluable importance, of the mundane and the ordinary. I am not suggesting humanists fail to ritualize major life developments and challenges; rather, I am arguing even these rituals must remain committed to the importance of the mundane, and in this way provide means by which to appreciate (as individuals and in communities) the wonders of everyday life. This is one of the strong contributions humanists can make to social existence—an unwillingness to look beyond the stuff of mundane existence, an unwillingness to demand the extraordinary as the only valuable marker of importance. This has been one of the lasting contributions of hip hop to the construction of cultural worlds. It is preoccupied with the ordinary, with the everyday and mundane patterns and moments of life; and, it seeks to provide a lexicon for discussing and moving through those moments. In this way, it tackles head-on the moments of discomfort, of paradox, of uncertainty that trouble—and by so doing it provides means by which to address the complexities of life. What such a move might allow is an earthly basis for our ethics. And, hip hop teaches valuable lessens—both positive and negative—concerning the people involved in these efforts and the sociocultural arrangements through means of which these people move through the world.

Bodies are real in that they live and die, and humanistic ethics should be concerned with the consequences and connotations of this realness. Our message, borrowing some cues from hip hop, might be the beauty of our ordinariness, the value of simple moments and events, and the need to appreciate this dimension of our existence—as individuals and in relationship. Doing so will trouble some humanists in that it means forgetting about some of the images of our godless liberalism. For example, on too many occasions, nontheists will proclaim that they do not see race; they do not give attention to difference in that way. They wear this proclamation like a blue ribbon—not realizing it is a statement representing a problem, not a solution. Antiblack racism and other modes of embodied discrimination aren't challenged and fought by ignoring them through colorblindness, as if difference must be cast as a problem. Rather, hip hop's approach to difference is much healthier, much more realistic in that hip hop culture understands difference not as a dilemma to solve but as a benefit that serves to enhance creativity, expand knowledge and perspective, and shape cultural connections in healthier and productive ways. So, see race. Humanists gain nothing by pretending not to see "colors." This illusion expends a lot of mental energy, generates a lot of social anxiety, and doesn't impress "racial minorities" (. . . minorities only if we fail to think globally).

3. Measured Realism

In place of outcome-driven systems, again, a humanist ethical outlook might locate success in the process of struggle. That is to say, continue to work. Humanists maintain this effort because they have the potential to effect/affect change, and they measure the value of their work not in terms of outcomes achieved but in the process of struggle itself. Regarding this, I am in agreement with ethicist, and senior fellow with the Institute for Humanist Studies, Sharon Welch. There is no foundation for moral action that guarantees individuals and groups will act in "productive" and liberating ways, nor that they will ultimately achieve their objectives. Therefore, as Welch argues, ethical activity is risky or dangerous because it requires operating without the certainty and security of a clearly articulated "product." This is a more sober—some might argue a less passionate—approach to ethics. It understands, what philosophers such as Michel Foucault noted with great accuracy and candor, that human relationships (with self, others, and the world) are messy, inconsistent, and thick with desires, contradictions, motives, and a hopeful hopelessness.

Humanistic ethical engagement should mirror the complexity and layered nature of the issues at hands.

As noted earlier, it currently stands, humanists, and traditional theists, share an unfortunate and unsupported posture of optimism. The reason for the optimism differs for these two camps: God for theists and science/reason for humanists. I am not pointing to the equation of God and forms of scientism (although this type of poor depiction of science does exist). Rather, I am suggesting that both traditional theists and humanists assume beneficial efforts to their actions—for them this is based on the balancing work done by the divinity; and for us it is premised on the assumption of science and reasonable thought as slow but steady resolutions to our problems. Isn't it in part because of this assumption so many humanists proclaim the demise of religion and the reign of reason? Both positions are too optimistic; but hip hop culture offers a more balanced perspective—something I have on many occasions referenced as measured realism.

Hip hop culture provides important lessons on the need for measured realism—a sense that human progress involves a paradox: advancement within a larger context of pain and misery. There must be awareness that human progress is not victim free, and it is not inevitable. That is to say, leave certainty to the theists; let their mythological protectors espouse overly optimistic pronouncements of future glory. Humanists should be in a better position than theists to see the world as it is and to undertake a much more mature posture toward work in the world. Humanists have not yet met the challenge, but they should: what is the look of ethical conduct when efforts are just as likely to fail as to succeed? Hip hop provides a way of thinking about this question, of moving through life without guaranteed outcomes. Like hip hop culture, humanists might learn to embrace the tragic quality of life and take from it a sobering regard for both their potential and their shortcomings. From this approach we might just come to a better and deeper appreciation of humanity.

* * *

If You Want To Know More

Some readers will disagree with my assessment, and some will resist giving hip hop such a prominent role in our thinking. Even this disagreement, if seriously engaged and interrogated, might just point in the direction of new and creative approaches to humanist thought and efforts. My goal is merely to suggest the importance of a particular conversation, to point out the weak spots in humanist mechanisms for understanding and acting out humanism with regard to race/racism. And for those willing to entertain this conversation, those who are curious enough to want to know more, I end with a few suggested readings:

Asante, M. K. *It's Bigger Than Hip Hop: The Rise of the Post-Hip Hop Generation* (New York: St. Martin's Griffin, 2009).

Chang, Jeff. *Can't Stop Won't Stop: A History of the Hip-Hop Generation* (New York: Picador, 2005).

Cobb, William Jelani. *To the Break of Dawn: A Freestyle on the Hip Hop Aesthetic* (New York: New York University Press, 2008).

Dyson, Michael Eric. *Know What I Mean? Reflections on Hip Hop* (New York: Basic Civitas Books, 2010).

Foreman, Murray and Mark Anthony Neal, editors. *That's the Joint! The Hip-Hop Studies Reader* (New York: Routledge, 2004).

Foucault, Michel. *Ethics: Subjectivity and Truth*, edited by Paul Rabinow (New York: The New Press, 1997), 319.

George, Nelson. *Buppies, B-Boys, Baps & Bohos: Notes on Post-Soul Black Culture* (New York: HarperPerennial, 1994).

Jay Z. *Decoded* (New York: Spiegel & Grau, 2011).

Miller, Monica R. *Religion and Hip Hop* (New York: Routledge, 2013).

Neal, Mark Anthony. *Soul Babies: Black Popular Culture and the Post-Soul Aesthetic* (New York: Routledge, 2002).

Ogbar, Jeffrey O. G. *Hip-Hop Revolution: The Culture and Politics of Rap* (Lawrence, KS: University Press of Kansas, 2007).

Pinn, Anthony B. "Handlin Our Business," in *Noise and Spirit*, ed. Anthony B. Pinn (New York: New York University Press, 2003).

Rose, Tricia. *Black Noise: Rap Music and Black Culture in Contemporary America* (Middletown, CT: Wesleyan University Press, 1994).

Stoute, Steve. *The Tanning of America: How Hip-Hop Created a Culture That Rewrote the Rules of the New Economy* (New York: Avery, 2012).

Welch, Sharon. *A Feminist Ethic of Risk* (Minneapolis, MN: Fortress Press, 2000).

8

CONCLUSION

"Where do we go from here?" This is a question asked by Martin Luther King, Jr. It is the title to his final book, and here I use it as a way of ending this volume. What's your answer?

* * *

My concern with race and racism as fundamental to humanist thought and activism won't make sense to all. And that is okay. I don't labor under the illusion that racial justice will be a priority for all humanists; rather, I'm suggesting it should be a priority and, for those interested in tackling this issue, I've offered the rough outline of a way forward.

My suggestions, my effort to offer a map of sorts, a way to negotiate and navigate issues of race and racism, I hope, will provide useful food for thought for those interested in my brand of humanist activism; and, for those who move in a different direction, they might offer a sense of the expansive agenda that marks the humanist "movement."

Either way, humanists are given opportunity to gain perspective on what matters, to wrestle with the degree to which black lives mattering matters to humanists.

I think humanists owe their collective community at least this much. If race matters, as some of the rhetoric I hear within humanist circles suggests, its time to get serious about addressing issues of racial injustice. The "how do we appeal to racial minorities" is a self serving and "tired" conversation when it doesn't evolve into concrete and sustainable activity that is based on solid information and knowledge of the nature and meaning of racial difference.

Still, what's required within the "movement" is a hard conversation, and it will involve discontent. But what is an acceptable level of discontent, of discomfort? In a word, when does disagreement on racism as an agenda item (or particular approaches to racial justice work) allow for creative and productive conversation, or a diversification of objectives and goals? And, when does it point to a destructive situation? Is consensus necessary on racial justice issues, or is majority enough? That is to say, what is the acceptable level of disagreement on racial justice issues within the movement *before such disagreement produces complacency and stagnation*?

I suggest disagreement is for certain in that humanists come to issues of race from a variety of vantage points and with differing relationships to the acknowledgment of white privilege. So, disagreement will exist but what is necessary is the determination of benchmarks.

Various organizations can produce position papers, mission statements, and objectives. All this is important work; however, shouldn't these "white paper" pronouncements bend to need? These statements and documents don't reify, but they need to be responsive to changing circumstances and predicaments. If these missions, objectives, etc., are organic, they will be responsive to the changing contexts in which humanists find themselves. Continued racial violence and injustice marks out one of these moments of need. How will humanists respond?

More than two decades ago, philosopher Cornel West wrote the book *Race Matters* (1994), which went on to become a *New York Times* bestseller. That book captured the imagination of a significant number of people and pushed them to think through their racial assumptions. In it he chronicles the nature, meaning, and function of race in the United States and offers ideas that push beyond dehumanizing practices and policies. Long before West wrote that book, sociologist and historian W. E. B. Du Bois' *Souls of Black Folk* (1903) made the

United States aware of the integral nature of race to life. He said, as I noted earlier in this book, the problem of the twentieth century is the problem of the color line, and more than a century later this, sadly, remains the case in very similar ways—e.g., restrictions on life options for racial minorities, violence against "black" bodies, nationalism that seeks to restrict access to this country and that projects as a problem anyone not easily identified as "white."

The problem of racial injustice has been persistent, although its form has shifted and changed in certain ways over time. And these modes of racial injustice have been matched with efforts to address these problems.

Most recently, the "Black Lives Matter" movement has gained something of a foothold on the popular imagination of the nation. But not all of this energy has been positive. Some have attempted to paint this movement as bigotry, reverse racism, or in general divisive because it advances one group's importance over others—as if not all lives matter. That's right, as I discussed in an earlier chapter, some have argued mistakenly it is more accurate, more progressive, and more justice-minded to promote a different slogan: "All Lives Matter." This, however, clouds the issue by recentering the conversation around those who have felt less of racism's sting. In short, it denies the impact of racism on certain populations and instead suggests whites suffer too and so talk of black lives mattering is really counterproductive. Put differently, this thinking goes, singling out African Americans promotes a problem of exclusion rather than solving a problem. Yet, it becomes much harder to address racial injustice when victims of racial injustice are sidelined by general claims to the human condition—apples and oranges.

It is my hope that humanists will get this right. Again, I want humanists to recognize that replacing "black lives matter" with "all lives matter" doesn't allow clear thinking on racial discrimination because it denies the existence of white privilege. It concerns itself with maintaining the comfort of the majority population, making certain it doesn't feel challenged.

The fact is that the humanity, the full importance, of white Americans has never been in question in a serious or sustained way—certainly not in a large-scale death-dealing manner. It has been assumed that white lives matter. Hence, "all lives matter" is misguided in that it fails to come to grips with the racial structure of life in the United States and the ways in which this structure advantages some and disadvantages some. Justice involves recognizing this inequality and correcting it.

Michelle Alexander's *The New Jim Crow* points out the manner in which the prison system works in concert with structures of racial injustice. And she highlights the consequences of black bodies confined and rendered docile in ways that point well beyond the consequences of law and order. Justice isn't blind. And the highly publicized death of African Americans in connection with law enforcement officers should serve to further highlight the devastating consequences of racial injustice. Still, for some theists and humanists, the jury is out, so to speak. Maybe the police were right to kill? Sure, deadly force might be necessary at times, but do these circumstances constitute such times? Or, does race have something to do with these situations? Were these black bodies assumed to be threatening because of what race and the bodies of racial minorities have come to mean and constitute in the United States? Color still matters.

Perhaps some who read this book will put it down unaffected by my arguments and suggestions. Others, I hope, will find it harder to be neutral on the question of racial justice and strategies for involvement. And, finally, I hope, as a consequence of something said in these pages, many will come to find more importance in pushing beyond "all lives matter" to more strategic work to end racial injustice.

Still, the nature of the response doesn't hide the fact humanists have reached a critical moment in the humanist "movement". There are pressing issues such as race/racism that demand attention. The content and scope of life in the United States rest in significant ways on how this ongoing challenge of racial injustice is addressed. Mindful of this, it's important to have some sense of what to do and what not to do.

* * *

If You Want to Know More

I'll end this final chapter as I've ended all the previous chapters—with a list of readings for those who want more information.

Alexander, Michelle. *The New Jim Crow: Mass Incarceration in the Age of Colorblindness* (New York: The New Press, 2012).

Allen, Theodore W. *The Invention of the White Race, Volume 1: Racial Oppression and Social Control* (New York: Verso, 2014).

Allen, Theodore W. *The Invention of the White Race, Volume 2: Racial Oppression and Social Control* (New York: Verso, 2014).

Bonilla-Silva, Eduardo. *Racism without Racists: Color-Blind Racism and the Persistence of Racial Inequality in America* (Lanham, MD: Rowman & Littlefield, 2013).

Cohen, Cathy J. *Democracy Remixed: Black Youth and the Future of American Politics* (New York: Oxford University Press, 2010).

Collins, Patricia Hill. *From Black Power to Hip Hop: Racism, Nationalism, and Feminism* (Philadelphia, PA: Temple University Press, 2006).

Dawson, Michael C. *Blacks In and Out of the Left* (Cambridge, MA: Harvard University Press, 2013).

Hutchinson, Sikivu. *Godless Americana: Race & Religious Rebels* (Los Angeles, CA: Infidel Books, 2013).

Marable, Manning. *Race, Reform, and Rebellion: The Second Reconstruction and Beyond in Black America, 1945–2006* (Oxford, MS: University Press of Mississippi, 2007).

Molina, Natalia. *How Race Is Made in America: Immigration, Citizenship, and the Historical Power of Racial Scripts* (Berkeley, CA: University of California Press, 2014).

Mora, G. Cristina. *Making Hispanics: How Activists, Bureaucrats, and Media Constructed a New American* (Chicago, IL: University of Chicago Press, 2014).

Omi, Michael and Howard Winant. *Racial Formation in the United States* (New York: Routledge, 2014).

Roithmayr, Daria. *Reproducing Racism: How Everyday Choices Lock in White Advantage* (New York: New York University Press, 2014).

Taylor, Keeanga-Yamahtaa. *From #BlackLivesMatter to Black Liberation* (New York: Haymarket Books, 2016).

Theoharis, Jeanne and Komozi Woodard, editors. *Groundwork: Local Black Freedom Movements in America* (New York: New York University Press, 2005).

West, Cornel. *Race Matters* (Boston: Beacon Press, 1994).

ABOUT THE AUTHOR

* * *

Anthony B. Pinn is the Agnes Cullen Arnold Professor of Humanities, professor of religion, and director of the Center for Engaged Research and Collaborative Learning at Rice University. He is the first African American full professor to hold an endowed chair in the history of Rice University. He is also director of research for the Institute for Humanist Studies and a member of the Board of Directors for the American Humanist Association. His numerous books include *The End of God-Talk: An African-American Humanist Theology* and *Writing God's Obituary: How a Good Methodist Became a Better Atheist*, as well as the novel *The New Disciples*. He lives in Houston.